PRAISE FOR

# MY SISTERS THE SAINTS

"A beautiful and inspiring story of a woman's deep faith and the saints who became her sisters along the path to her answered prayers."

—**Mary Higgins Clark**, worldwide bestselling novelist

"Colleen Carroll Campbell has encountered most of the challenges confronting young women today—balancing dating, courtship, and marriage with a successful career; caring for a parent with Alzheimer's; dealing with infertility—but she hasn't faced these challenges alone. In *My Sisters the Saints*, Campbell introduces us to the women who helped her along the way—women like Teresa of Ávila, Thérèse of Lisieux, Edith Stein, and, of course, the Blessed Virgin Mary. Completely contemporary and totally timeless, *My Sisters the Saints* is an engaging spiritual memoir and the perfect guidebook for anyone who is looking for a companion to help her navigate life's sometimes difficult and confusing journey."

—**Cardinal Timothy Dolan**, archbishop of New York

"In this fascinating memoir, Colleen Carroll Campbell recounts her discovery of kinship with six great women saints at crucial junctures on her journey through life. *My Sisters the Saints* is the story of how a thoroughly modern woman drew inspiration and strength from her spiritual 'sisters' while struggling with the mysteries of life, love, illness, and death in today's world. This lovely and highly readable book will touch many lives."

—**Mary Ann Glendon**, former U.S. ambassador to the Vatican, Harvard Law School professor, and president of the Pontifical Academy of Social Sciences

"Fully alive, authentically feminine, making a serious contribution to culture—and faithfully Catholic? In the minds of many still, an unlikely combination, at best. In *My Sisters the Saints*, Colleen Carroll Campbell recounts her own life's story and the poignant struggles she encounters in fulfilling her dreams as an author, journalist, cultural commentator, and woman. Campbell's stories will resonate in the heart of every woman challenged by today's culture and blessed with even a scintilla of faith. You won't put this book down until you have finished the last page. And as you read, you will hold your breath in hopefulness experiencing with Colleen the grippingly real decisions in this woman's life—both big and small—the response to which ultimately define who one is as a person. . . . Thank you, Colleen, for the courage to tell your own story. It makes an important and unique contribution to the lives of women by giving flesh to the beauty, meaning, and purposes of human life and human love lived open to the mystery of God."

—**Mother Agnes Mary Donovan, S.V.**, superior general, Sisters of Life

"Colleen Carroll Campbell is one of the finest writers on the American Catholic scene, and *My Sisters the Saints* shows her heart, her skill, and her keen intelligence at their best. This is a wonderful, engaging personal memoir and a great witness of faith."

—**Charles J. Chaput, O.F.M. Cap.**, archbishop of Philadelphia

"This book is a powerful description of the long struggle Colleen Carroll Campbell had to undergo to go back to peace, to give God the place that belongs to him: the first. The lesson she learned is not to be forgotten: When in need, let us remember that we have brothers and sisters in heaven whose lives and sufferings teach the way to peace."

—**Alice von Hildebrand**, author of *The Privilege of Being a Woman* and *The Soul of a Lion: The Life of Dietrich von Hildebrand*

"Colleen Carroll Campbell is a genuine icon of the 'new feminism' called for by Blessed John Paul II. She has been on a long journey in search of the true meaning of women's liberation and in *My Sisters the Saints* she tells the story of how six women mystics and her own personal trials and triumphs have helped her find that liberation at the foot of the cross. Refreshing, well written, down to earth, and a joy to read (I'd often find myself grinning as I read it), Colleen has given us a sincere gift: not only the gift of her intellect and skill as a writer, but, more important, she has opened her heart and given us the sincere gift of herself. Stop wondering whether you should read this book. You should!"

—**Christopher West**, author of *Fill These Hearts* and fellow at the Theology of the Body Institute

"In *My Sisters the Saints*, Colleen Carroll Campbell shows how in our attentiveness to the saints we learn not only about the Lord and the way of life he imparts, but also how we discern the most important truths about who we are and the purpose for which we have been created. *My Sisters the Saints* brilliantly illuminates how the Christian life cannot be understood as an abstraction, but shows its radiant form in our friendship with heavenly companions who meet us in the real events and concrete circumstances of our lives."

—**Father Robert Barron**, author and host of *Catholicism* and founder of Word on Fire Catholic Ministries

"In *My Sisters the Saints*, Colleen Carroll Campbell has liberated these great historical heroines from dusty altarpieces and stone effigies and has brought them into the new millennium. Through her literary portraits, they become sure-footed guides through the modern-day spiritual minefield of the 'hook-up' culture, the difficulties of commitment and family, and the ever-present reality of suffering and loss. By the end, one finds oneself with six new girlfriends whose wit, common sense, and faith transcend any age."

—**Elizabeth Lev**, art historian and author of *The Tigress of Forli*

"From her own life's story, Colleen Carroll Campbell has depicted a spiritual journey marked by waiting for and letting go. She learns of motherhood—both spiritual and biological—from the holy women whose lives reflect her own journey back to her. Her personal story teaches a universal lesson: living free is different from being in control. This is a moving and beautiful book."

—**Cardinal Francis George, O.M.I.**, archbishop of Chicago

"The saints undo the world—for by their sheer existence, they tell us we may have gotten it wrong: all our conventions, all our agreements, all our correctnesses and easy thoughts are no help when things come crashing in. In troubled times, Colleen Carroll Campbell found herself by reading the lives of the great women saints. And you might find your own self, reading Campbell's *My Sisters the Saints*."

—**Joseph Bottum**, author of *An Anxious Age*

"With this intimate memoir, Colleen Carroll Campbell gives a moving witness to the 'cloud of witnesses' celebrated in sacred scripture."

—**Dawn Eden**, author of *My Peace I Give You* and *The Thrill of the Chaste*

"This is an inspiring and insightful account of one young woman's journey through the challenges of contemporary culture, the ups and downs of life, and her encounter with the wisdom of the saints. This is the story of a journey told with refreshing honesty and great insight that will benefit many."

—**Ralph Martin**, author of *The Fulfillment of All Desire* and president of Renewal Ministries

"*St. Louis Post-Dispatch* columnist Campbell (*The New Faithful: Why Young Adults Are Embracing Christian Orthodoxy*, 2002) relates a provocative life story centered on her experiences as a woman in the Catholic Church. Intertwined with the author's tale is her autobiography as a reader, her experiences with books by and about various saints who have deeply influenced every aspect of her life. . . . Throughout the book, Campbell describes how various women saints helped her understand her situation and move ahead. . . . A charming and instructive communion with saintly sisters."

—***Kirkus Reviews***

"Thoughtful and gracious, Campbell's story will serve as an inspiration for many young women who are attempting to straddle two very different worlds—the sacred and the profane—in a society with little patience for subtlety or complexity."

—***Booklist***

# MY SISTERS THE SAINTS

# MY SISTERS THE SAINTS

A Spiritual Memoir

COLLEEN CARROLL CAMPBELL

NEW YORK

Published in the United States by Image, an imprint of the Crown Publishing Group, a division of Random House LLC, New York, a Penguin Random House Company.
www.crownpublishing.com

IMAGE is a registered trademark of Random House LLC and the "I" colophon is a trademark of Random House LLC.

Originally published in hardcover in the United States by Image, New York, an imprint of the Crown Publishing Group, a division of Random House LLC, in 2012.

*Grateful acknowledgment is made to the following for permission to reprint previously published material:*

ICS Publications: excerpts from "Ethos of Woman's Professions," "Spirituality of the Christian Woman," "Vocations of Man and Woman," "Principles of Women's Education," and "Women's Value in National life" from *Essays on Woman: The Collected Works of Edith Stein, Revised Second Edition, Volume 2,* edited by Lucy Gelber and Romaeus Leuven, translated by Freda Mary Oben, copyright © 1987, 1996 Washington Province of Discalced Carmelites. Reprinted with the permission of ICS Publications, 2131 Lincoln Road NE, Washington, DC 20002-1199, www.icspublications.org

ICS Publications: excerpts from *Story of a Soul: The Autobiography of St. Thérèse of Lisieux, Third Edition,* translated by John Clarke, O.C.D., copyright © 1996 Washington Province of Discalced Carmelites. Reprinted with permission of ICS Publications, 2131 Lincoln Road NE, Washington, DC 20002-1199, www.icspublications.org

The Mother Teresa Center: excerpts from *Mother Teresa: Come Be My Light: The Private Writings of the Saint of Calcutta,* edited and with commentary by Brian Kolodiejchuk, M.C. (New York: Doubleday, 2007). Copyright © 2007 by The Mother Teresa Center. Reprinted with the permission of The Mother Teresa Center.

Sheed & Ward, Inc.: excerpts from *The Complete Works of Saint Teresa of Jesus, Volume 1: General Introduction, Life, Spiritual Relations,* translated and edited by Edgar Allison Peers. Reprinted with the permission of Sheed & Ward, Inc., Lanham, Maryland, https://rowman.com/Partners

Library of Congress Cataloging-in-Publication Data
Campbell, Colleen Carroll
My sisters the saints / Colleen Carroll Campbell. — 1st ed.
p. cm.
1. Campbell, Colleen Carroll. 2. Catholics—United States—Biography. 3. Christian women saints. 4. Women in the Catholic Church. 5. Feminist theology. I. Title.
BX4705.C245887 A3 2012
282.092—dc23
[B]
2012006683

ISBN 978-0-7704-3651-3
eBook ISBN 978-0-7704-3650-6

Printed in the United States of America

*Book design by Maria Elias*
*Cover design by Rebecca Lown*
*Cover photography: Julie Mcinnes/Getty Images*

2 4 6 8 10 9 7 5 3 1

First Paperback Edition

*To John,*
*with admiration for all you are,*
*gratitude for all you do,*
*and love with all my heart*

# Contents

## A Note to the Reader

This is the story of a journey, a personal search for insight and peace that began with that age-old, seductively simple question: Is this all there is?

In my life that question took a contemporary and feminine twist when it first forced itself upon me one autumn morning midway through my college years. Reeling from a rough night, I found myself puzzled by the gulf between the boisterous party scene that had once captivated me and the menacing emptiness that consumed me in quieter moments. That puzzlement marked the start of a fifteen-year quest to understand the meaning of my feminine identity in light of my Christian faith and a culture shaped by modern feminism.

The spiritual journey that ensued led me to unexpected places, from the baths of Lourdes and ruins of Auschwitz to the Oval Office and the papal palace. Along the way, I wrestled with the quintessential dilemmas of my generation: confusion over the sexual chaos of the hookup culture, tension between my dueling desires for professional success and committed love, ambivalence about the demands of marriage and parenthood, and anguish over a beloved parent's descent into illness and my own confrontation with a devastating diagnosis.

Dissatisfied by pat answers offered by both secular feminists and their antifeminist critics, I found grace and inspiration from an unexpected source: spiritual friendships with six women saints. In the lives and writings of Teresa of Ávila, Thérèse of Lisieux, Faustina of Poland, Edith Stein of Germany, Mother Teresa of Calcutta, and Mary of Nazareth, I discovered kindred spirits. These women spoke to my deepest longings, guided me through my most wrenching decisions, and transformed my understanding of love and liberation.

You might think it odd that I speak of intimate friendships with women I have never met, women who have been dead for decades, centuries, even millennia. Once upon a time, I would have agreed. But that was before my journey began, before the joys, sorrows, and reversals chronicled in these pages convinced me of the living and powerful reality that is the communion of saints.

I hope the story of my journey, and the stories of the six holy women who guided me on my way, will encourage you to discover for yourself the consoling truth too often forgotten in our individualistic age: that the pilgrim who seeks God never travels alone.

# MY SISTERS THE SAINTS

1

# Party Girl

I still remember the sundress I was wearing that morning; it was black, scoop-necked, and short. Its thin fabric hung loosely on my frame, thanks to punishing daily workouts and a scrupulously fat-free diet, but I felt uncomfortably warm. Perched on the windowsill of our fourth-floor apartment, I dangled my legs in mid-air. I couldn't believe it was late October. Milwaukee was usually chillier by now, already beginning its slouch toward the interminable Wisconsin winter. As the sun baked my skin, still bronze from dutiful visits to the tanning salon, I squinted and squirmed. I didn't want to be here.

I had just come home from the night before and was suffering the start of a monster hangover. My head throbbed and my itchy skin begged for a shower. Tom Petty was wailing from the stereo speakers: *I'm tired of myself/Tired of this town.* In the parking lot below, I spotted empty beer bottles and stray partiers trudging home from after-hours revelry and drunken couplings.

Behind me, a couple of my still-drunk college roommates were singing and dancing like banshees before the large open windows in our living room. The place stank of stale beer and cigarettes from a party we had thrown the first week of our junior year and from the many rowdy weekends that had followed. Although we were only two months into the fall semester, our brand-new apartment complex already bore vomit stains on its hallway rugs and fist-sized holes in its plaster walls—proof of how most of its student tenants spent their weekends.

I liked this vantage point, looking down from a distant perch. It made me feel removed from the chaos. I always had felt somewhat separate from the campus party scene, even as I indulged in many of its pleasures. I was a scholarship student carrying a near-perfect GPA, on track to land a prestigious summer internship in Washington, DC, and serving as editor-in-chief of the campus magazine. I had a résumé packed with honor society memberships and evidence of a properly raised social consciousness.

As for the Catholic faith that had dominated my life in elementary and high school, well, that had taken a backseat to other priorities. I still considered myself a better-than-average Catholic. Since my freshman year, I had been active in all the right social justice organizations, devoting at least one afternoon or evening each week to busing tables at a nearby homeless shelter or feeding vagrants through a campus meals-on-wheels program. I attended Mass every Sunday. When it came to sex, I abided by the letter of the law I had been taught in my Catholic home—no sex outside marriage—though not its spirit. My true zeal was reserved for more concrete concerns, like obsessing over my body to make sure I stayed thin and fit. Unlike the other party girls who devoured late-night pizzas and hid their beer guts under loose-fitting flannel, I told myself, I was in control.

But lately my pride at compartmentalizing my life so completely—being a good girl on Sunday morning and a wild one on Saturday night—had begun to give way to something new, a dawning realization that I was as immersed in the chaos as anyone. Maybe I was even worse, because I was leading a double life. At least the potbellied partiers down the hall were consistent. They were not spending their lives keeping up appearances and juggling personas, playing the role of perfectionist honor student for one crowd and reckless reveler for another.

Looking back over my shoulder into our apartment, I saw my roommates sprawled on the couch, now drowsy and listless after a long night of carousing. I realized that living with them, and living like them, no longer made me happy. Nor did my relationship with the brooding rugby player who routinely rounded up his friends to meet me at whatever bar my friends and I were patronizing that night. I could not call our random meetings dates, and I could not call him my boyfriend. There were no names for such romantic entanglements, no rules of engagement, and most of the time my friends and I had no idea what to make of the men in our lives. We were unconstrained by customs of courtship or social norms. We could do whatever we wanted. Yet the awkwardness, confusion, and disappointment that marked our encounters with men made me wonder: Was our unfettered freedom just a trap in disguise?

This was not what I had envisioned when I set off for college. I had thought I would spend my Saturday nights discussing Aquinas over coffee and dating the kind of men who send roses, open car doors, and pay for dinner. I ran into a few of those men during my college years, but I had become so inured to the anti-dating ethos of campus life by then that I quickly dropped them and rejoined my friends on the party circuit.

Returning my gaze to the bleak scene beneath my window, I realized how much things had changed—how much I had changed—since I first arrived at my freshman dorm that muggy August move-in day. I had lost something. I didn't know what it was or how to get it back. I only knew that this aching emptiness in the pit of my stomach had grown unbearable.

Suddenly aware that I was shivering, I swung my legs back into the living room. I stood up, slammed the window shut, and strode past my roommates, now sleeping soundly despite the ear-splitting music.

It was time to shower, to eat, to put on something warmer.

It was time for a change.

## Blame It on Patriarchy

I did not know it at the time, but I was taking the first steps on a journey upon which many women in my generation have embarked, women asking the same questions that I asked that morning: What is the source of that gnawing sensation inside me, and why does my pursuit of pleasure and success only intensify it? Is it true that there are no real differences between the sexes, or does my femininity—and female body—have something to do with my desires and discontent? If the key to my fulfillment as a woman lies in maximizing my sexual allure, racking up professional accomplishments, and indulging my appetites while avoiding commitment, why has following that advice left me dissatisfied? Why do my friends and I spend so many hours fretting that we are not thin enough, not successful enough, simply not enough? If this is liberation, why am I so miserable?

About a year after I first began pondering these questions, I enrolled in a course on feminist thought. I knew that the women's liberation movement had played a large role in shaping the world that my friends and I inhabited, so I wanted to know what its leaders said about what makes a woman distinct from a man and how a woman can find freedom and fulfillment.

I had never given feminism much thought before that course. It was simply the air I breathed as a girl growing up in the 1970s and 1980s and coming of age in the 1990s. Like most women in my generation, I was wary of associating myself too closely with the passé image of man-hating, bra-burning radical feminists. Yet I vigorously supported the basic feminist premise of equal rights for women. I was drawn from a young age to stories about heroines and suffragettes and had embraced the feminist conventional wisdom that I should spend the first few decades of adulthood establishing myself in a career and squeeze in marriage and motherhood when I found time. As for differences between the sexes, I always sensed that they existed but avoided acknowledging them aloud, lest that acknowledgment be perceived as a sign of weakness or an excuse for underachievement.

Now I was ready to take a closer look at sex differences and feminism itself. In my course, I eagerly devoured the first few readings we were given, manifestos of early feminists who demanded equal educational opportunities, the right to vote, and humane working and living conditions even as they acknowledged the uniqueness of women. As the semester progressed and we worked our way through more contemporary feminists, though, I grew increasingly uneasy with the theorists we were reading. Many seethed with resentment at men. Others raged against their own femininity. The more I read, the more I found myself bristling at their views of men and women, marriage and motherhood, and God.

I had met my share of chauvinists, and I knew that I enjoyed opportunities denied to earlier generations of women, including the chance to take courses like this one. I also knew that feminism comes in many forms. Yet most of the feminist writers we studied struck me as shrill and hyperbolic, with their denunciations of housewives and stay-at-home mothers as "parasites," as Simone de Beauvoir called them, or inmates in a "comfortable concentration camp," as Betty Friedan put it. It bothered me that so many theorists we read succumbed to one of two extremes: Either they allowed their insistence on the equality of men and women to obscure the differences between the sexes, or they allowed their emphasis on the differences between the sexes to obscure the equality of men and women.

Neither extreme made much sense to me. Nor did I find in what I was reading any viable blueprints for happiness in the real world. A friend who took the course with me felt the same way. "If all else fails," she would groan as we walked out of class together, "blame it on patriarchy." She was a convinced atheist and I was a churchgoing Christian, but we agreed that the theories we were learning did not address our most pressing questions and concerns.

There was another problem with the secular feminist thinkers we studied. For all of their criticism of men's fixation on money, sex, power, and status, most of these women obsessed over the very same things. They harped on which perks and privileges men had that women did not. I could see the logic behind some of their complaints, but their materialistic worldview felt stifling. There was no transcendent horizon, few references to truth, beauty, goodness, or God. It was all about what you could see, taste, and touch. I found nothing that spoke to the thirst inside me that material pleasures had failed to slake.

## An Open Door

Near the end of the first semester of my senior year, I found myself standing in the back of the cavernous neo-Gothic Church of the Gesu on Marquette University's campus, wondering where to turn next for answers. It was a Sunday night and I had dragged my new graduate student boyfriend to the "drive-through" 6 P.M. Mass. It was a popular one, tailored to the many students too hungover to make it to morning Mass, too apathetic to worship for a full hour, and too guilt-ridden to skip their Sunday obligation altogether.

Attending Mass with a boyfriend was new for me. Having a boyfriend also was new, as I had dismissed my last real boyfriend midway through the first semester of my freshman year. This current relationship had taken root not because of any great reformation on my part but simply due to my growing boredom with the campus party scene, from which our weekly dates—at real restaurants, complete with real conversations—relieved me.

Like nearly every man with whom I had been involved in the previous three years, this one was a nominal Catholic but practical atheist. On this particular night, he initially had agreed to attend Mass with me, then begged me to skip it and lounge on the couch with him instead. In the end he succeeded only in making me fifteen minutes late for a thirty-minute Mass.

There were no seats left by the time we stepped through Gesu's massive wooden doors, so we huddled in the back of the nave with the rest of the stragglers. As my boyfriend leaned in to whisper a wisecrack to me, I brushed him away and strained to see over the crowd and catch a glimpse of the altar. We had missed the Gospel reading, missed the priest's abbreviated homily, and now he was well into the Eucharistic prayer. Feeling flushed and irritable, I wondered how my once-ardent childhood faith had been reduced to this. Was there a connection between the malaise that had settled over my spiritual life and the nagging discontent I had first noticed on that window ledge?

It had been a year since I recognized that emptiness, and I still had no clue what to do about it. My feminist theory class had not helped. Nor had the series of cosmetic changes I had made recently: switching apartments and roommates, cultivating a more temperate group of friends and an older boyfriend, devoting more attention to my freelance writing career and an application for a Rhodes Scholarship and less attention to aerobics classes and barhopping. I had worked hard to get my life into better order, to make myself into the kind of woman who indulges her desires with discretion and never feels as lost and desolate as I did that October morning.

Still, I could not shake that aching feeling in the pit of my stomach. As I stood in the back of church that night, I realized that my lingering melancholy might be connected to the intimacy with God that I had abandoned shortly after arriving at college.

For more than three years, I had given God the scraps of my time and attention, put him last on my list of sources to turn to for answers and fulfillment. Now, after having chased my every whim and put everything and everyone before God, my spiritual life consisted of just that: scraps.

When Mass ended a few minutes later, I found myself caught up in the herd of students barreling down the church stairs and into the frigid night air. My boyfriend and I were halfway down the snow-lined block before I stopped and turned to him.

"I need to go back into church," I told him. "I left something behind."

"Okay," he said. "I'll go with you."

"No!" I snapped, a little louder than I intended. "Just go ahead. I'll catch up with you later."

His brow furrowed and I could feel him staring at me as I turned and began pushing through the crowd to get back inside. I probably looked crazy, and I didn't care. My eyes blurred with tears as I fought my way up the stairs, this time moving against the tide of surging bodies. When I finally cleared the crowd and stepped inside the empty, unlit nave, I did not quite know what to do. Feeling a mixture of anger and despair, I knelt in a nearby pew and let the darkness engulf me.

I lingered there for fifteen minutes, allowing myself to feel the full force of that hollowness I had been trying to paper over and outrun for more than a year. So this is it, I thought, as the tears ran down my cheeks. This is life without God. Something about the frank desperation of it all felt good. I was no longer sleepwalking. I finally felt awake.

Words slowly began to come, silent pleas from a soft, vulnerable voice I had not heard in years: "I want you, Lord. I want to know you. I know there's more to life than this. There's more to you than this. There must be. But you have to show me. I'm opening my eyes, finally, but you have to show yourself to me."

I paused, waiting for a thunderbolt or a warm wave of consolation. I got neither.

Minutes passed and my mind began to wander. I found myself thinking about my parents, about their various trials and tribulations through the years. They never had enough money; they were always struggling to make ends meet thanks to jobs in the charitable sector and with the church; and lately Dad had been acting particularly odd, forgetting things and driving Mom crazy around the house. Yet they were joyful together, full of laughter and love and confidence about the future despite their crises. They always seemed sure that God would care for their needs. And in the end, it seemed, he always did. I envied their deep-down, joyful peace. I wanted it for myself. I had experienced it throughout my childhood, but now it seemed to have disappeared. How could I get it back?

I thought of the spiritual disciplines I had seen my parents cultivate through the years: faithful attendance at daily Mass, daily contemplative prayer, and regular reading of scripture and spiritual books. I thought: I can do that. I will do that. I won't tell anyone, of course; I don't want anyone thinking I'm a religious nut. I'll seek God again after all these years, but I'll do it on my terms—in secret.

I waited in the silence for some divine confirmation of my resolution, but nothing came. So I wiped my eyes with the back of my hand, stepped out of the pew, and shuffled down the church stairs for a second time. I strolled out into the black November night with no answers, no miracle solutions, none of the can-do energy that had spurred me on after my earlier experience on the window ledge. I felt nothing at all, aside from a vague sense of anticipation. I had opened the door to God. The next move was his.

## Saints and Superstars

Over the next few weeks I haphazardly hewed to my new resolutions, catching a weekday Mass here and a few minutes of prayer there, with precious little spiritual reading. My life did not otherwise change. I still partied every weekend, ranked my social life far ahead of spiritual pursuits, and continued an increasingly intense relationship with my boyfriend despite my sense that it was pulling me farther from God.

When Christmas break rolled around, I found myself marooned with my parents in St. Louis, a city they had moved to after I graduated from high school and in which I knew no one. Boredom as much as spiritual longing led me to accept my father's invitation to join him each day for Mass at Saint Louis University's Saint Francis Xavier College Church, a neo-Gothic structure in the heart of the city that looked a lot like Marquette's Gesu. Unlike the spectacular sanctuary above it, the underground Chapel of Our Lady where Dad and I attended 5:15 P.M. Mass was a simple space with a sole wooden crucifix and a few dozen wood-and-wicker chairs facing a plain altar. Its sparseness seemed to mirror something happening inside both of us, a stripping process spawned for Dad by his recent retirement from work as a lay hospital chaplain and for me by my experience in Gesu a month earlier.

During our drives home from Mass, Dad would rave about

the biography he was reading, Marcelle Auclair's *Saint Teresa of Ávila.* On Christmas Day he gave me a copy. "It makes Teresa come alive," Dad told me, leaning forward in his chair as he shook the fat red paperback before me, trying to convey its value. "Reading it, you feel like you really know her."

I thanked him and tried to look interested as I scanned its staid-looking back cover. Dad probably knew that I was more excited about the sweaters and jewelry my mom had bought me and the bouquet of red roses my boyfriend had sent. He was right. I still had a fairly anemic appetite for spiritual reading, and this book looked far too dry for vacation reading. I planned to toss it onto the same dust-collecting shelf where I had relegated all the other religious books Mom and Dad had given me since I left for college.

It wasn't that I didn't appreciate their gifts. It was just that they were always gushing about their favorite saints: Teresa of Ávila, John of the Cross, Thérèse of Lisieux, and dozens of others. Dad and Mom read the saints' lives again and again, swapped dog-eared tomes about mystical prayer, and cheered whenever one bought the other some obscure book on one of their beloved holy people. From my earliest years, I remember seeing my parents huddled together, talking animatedly about new saints they had discovered or new insights on scripture that they had gleaned from people they referred to simply as "John," "Teresa" or "the Little Flower." Images of Jesus, Mary, and Joseph adorned every room in our home, and our bookshelves bulged with titles by and about saints and servants of God. The names on the spines were as familiar as old friends: Augustine, Ignatius, Francis de Sales, Francis of Assisi, Mother Teresa, Dorothy Day.

As a little girl, I had shared my parents' attraction to the saints, particularly women saints. Sainthood seemed to me to be the premier career choice. Rather than being merely a successful writer or actress or artist or lawyer, I could be something infinitely more glorious: a person who enjoyed eternal bliss with God in heaven while being revered as a Christian superstar on earth. If I were a saint, I reasoned, I could someday do favors for my family and friends when they petitioned me from earth to intercede with Jesus on their behalf. And I could enjoy a level of renown far superior to the fleeting fame of a Hollywood starlet or bestselling author, since the esteem enjoyed by saints lasts for centuries, even millennia.

My favorite childhood saint was Rose of Lima, a stunningly beautiful Peruvian woman whose pint-sized biography in my children's book of saints was tattered from repeated readings. Rose practiced extreme penances to conquer her vanity, including rubbing her face raw with pepper so it would not inspire so many compliments. That struck me as a little creepy, but I admired Rose's love for Jesus and zeal for combating a character flaw that I recognized in myself. I also liked the sound of her name, which is why I chose Rose as my patron saint for confirmation in eighth grade.

Like so much else in my spiritual life, my interest in the saints had fizzled in college. Fixated as I was on final exams and Friday-night plans, the last thing I wanted to read was some sugary tale about a snow-pure saint whose biggest sin paled in comparison with what transpired in the first five minutes of the average kegger. But Christmas-break boredom can make a college student do desperate things, and that December it made me crack open a forty-five-year-old biography of Teresa of Ávila.

Once I did, I was hooked.

## Meeting Teresa

The story of Teresa de Cepeda y Ahumada begins in the early sixteenth century, with a pious Spanish childhood saturated by God's presence. Willful, bright, and passionate, little Teresa dreamed of sainthood and even convinced her younger brother to run away from home with her so they could fight the Moors and die as martyrs. Their plan was foiled by a vigilant uncle, who spotted the pair leaving the city. So the aspiring contemplatives settled for building homemade hermitages instead, where they prayed and read stories of the saints together.

As Teresa grew into adolescence, her beauty and vivacious personality blossomed, but her religious zeal withered. She lost her mother in her early teens and started spending more time with cousins whose superficiality fanned the flames of her vanity. A party girl with the gift of gab and no shortage of male admirers, Teresa became preoccupied by beauty regimens, romance novels, fashion, and gossip.

Her devout father noticed the change in his daughter and sent her away to a convent boarding school, where her faith began to flourish again. Although she initially felt little attraction to religious life, the idea of becoming a nun gradually grew on Teresa and she resolved to pursue it despite her father's objections. After returning home and enduring a debilitating, life-threatening illness for the remainder of her teen years, Teresa recovered and ran away from home again—this time to join a Carmelite convent.

The preoccupations with vanity, praise, and flirtations that had characterized Teresa's teen years resurfaced after she became a nun. Life in the convent was soft; sisters there freely mingled with men and women from the town, and the wealthier sisters enjoyed many of the same material comforts and perks they had known at home—from plush suites to in-room pets. Hailing from an aristocratic family and possessed of a keen ability to charm others, Sister Teresa of Jesus followed the relaxed rules of her order but focused her energy on winning honor from other people rather than honoring God. "I was fond of everything to do with the religious life," she writes in her autobiography, "but I could not bear anything which seemed to make me ridiculous. I delighted in being thought well of."

Teresa paid little attention to avoiding sin aside from the most obvious offenses, happy to take the advice of lax confessors who told her not to sweat her faults. She performed external acts of devotion "with more vanity than spirituality," she writes, "for I always wanted things to be done very meticulously and well." Her prayer life soon withered. As she recounts,

> I began, then, to indulge in one pastime after another, in one vanity after another and in one occasion of sin after another. Into so many and such grave occasions of sin did I fall, and so far was my soul led astray by all these vanities, that I was ashamed to return to God and to approach Him in the intimate friendship which comes from prayer. This shame was increased by the fact that, as my sins grew in number, I began to lose the pleasure and joy which I had been deriving from virtuous things. I saw very clearly, my Lord, that this was failing me because I was failing Thee.

After suffering a series of illnesses and the death of her father, Teresa encountered a devout Dominican priest who convinced her to resume her prayers and pay closer attention to her sins. She did the former, though not the latter, and the result was a torturous feeling of living in two worlds: "My life became full of trials, because by means of prayer I learned more and more about my faults. On the one hand, God was calling me. On the other, I was following the world. All the things of God gave me great pleasure, yet I was tied and bound to those of the world. . . . I spent many years in this way, and now I am amazed that a person could have gone on for so long without giving up either the one or the other."

Teresa spent nearly two decades locked in this dual existence, yearning for God yet clinging to the worldly pleasures, people-pleasing habits, and shallow conversations that kept him at a distance. A profound and frustrating emptiness gradually engulfed her as she grew weary of vacillating between her competing desires. She was living, she writes, "one of the most grievous kinds of life which I think can be imagined, for I had neither any joy in God nor any pleasure in the world. When I was in the midst of worldly pleasures, I was distressed by the remembrance of what I owed to God; when I was with God, I grew restless because of worldly affections."

A breakthrough finally came when Teresa was thirty-nine. She walked into the chapel one day and came face-to-face with a statue of the suffering Christ, bloodied and bound as he awaited his Crucifixion. The image startled Teresa. She found herself overcome with regret for the years she had wasted serving herself instead of God. "I felt as if my heart were breaking," Teresa recalls, "and I threw myself down beside him, shedding floods of tears and begging him to give me strength once for all so that I might not offend him." Although she had shed repentant tears before, this time was different "because I had quite lost trust in myself and was placing all my confidence in God." Teresa told Jesus that she would not get up from the floor until he had given her the help she needed. "And I feel sure that this did me good," she writes, "for from that time onward I began to improve."

Teresa's prayer life began to deepen, and her desire to spend time with God intensified. Around the same time, someone passed her a copy of Saint Augustine's *Confessions.* The spiritual autobiography of this fourth-century playboy-turned-saint who spent years struggling with sensuality and sinful habits resonated with her. She was particularly moved when she came upon Augustine's account of his spiritual turning point in the garden, where he heard a child's voice inviting him to "take and read" a nearby Bible. Augustine opened the book and read the first lines he saw, from Saint Paul's Letter to the Romans: "Let us conduct ourselves properly as in the day, not in orgies and drunkenness, not in promiscuity and licentiousness, not in rivalry and jealousy. But put on the Lord Jesus Christ, and make no provision for the desires of the flesh" (Rom. 13:13–14).

Augustine did not need to read any further; he knew God intended those words for him. Reading his story, Teresa felt the same way. She writes, "It seemed as if the Lord were speaking in that way to me," welcoming her into the freedom from sin and intimate relationship with him that had eluded her for so long.

Teresa began to make swifter progress on her spiritual journey. Her prayer life grew richer and more rewarding, and her attachment to pleasure seeking and winning the admiration of others steadily declined. Her ascent to holiness did not happen overnight: The road to her famed prayer experiences, like her decades-long spiritual awakening itself, was paved with struggle. In the early years of her prayer life, Teresa writes, "I was more occupied in wishing my hour of prayer were over, and in listening whenever the clock struck, than in thinking of things that were good." She found that the times she persevered in prayer despite her natural inclination to do otherwise were those that left her with "more tranquility and happiness than at certain other times when I had prayed because I had wanted to."

Through her struggles, Teresa discovered the wisdom of the Catholic teaching that our bodies, and what we do with them, matter. She came to understand that while God wants us to treat our bodies with respect, excessive focus on perfecting our bodies or indulging their insatiable desires—including the desire to busy ourselves with good works to avoid the discomfort of solitude and silence—distances us from God. The same goes for social status, popularity, and professional achievement, things that are not evil in themselves but that can wreak spiritual havoc when we value them more than we value God.

Once Teresa broke free of such idols, she redirected to God the passion she had frittered away on the quest for material pleasures and social approval. Her intense love for Jesus and profound prayer life gave her the strength to launch a historic reform of her religious order, endure severe persecution from civil and religious authorities who resisted her efforts, and pen several classics of contemplative spirituality. Battling critics both inside and outside her order, Teresa refused to back down in her quest to transform her Carmelite convents from havens for spoiled socialites to places of genuine simplicity and prayer. She adhered faithfully to her religious vow of obedience, however, forgiving her detractors and attracting followers inspired by her to live for God alone.

By the time of her death, Teresa had established dozens of Discalced Carmelite convents, sparking a renewal of religious life that rippled across the Catholic Church and helped revitalize it in the wake of the Protestant Reformation. She became one of the church's greatest saints and mystics, a trailblazer in faith as well as works. In 1970, Pope Paul VI named her a Doctor of the Church, an honor previously granted only to men. The distracted, vain woman who spent the first four decades of her life obsessed with looking good in the eyes of others evolved into a spiritual powerhouse who heroically lived the words of her famous poem:

*Let nothing disturb you,*
*Let nothing frighten you,*
*All things are passing away:*
*God never changes.*
*Patience obtains all things.*
*Whoever has God lacks nothing;*
*God alone suffices.*

## A Desire Enkindled

Reading Teresa's story helped me understand for the first time why my parents had returned to her works so often and spoken of her with such affection. In Teresa, I found a woman of passion and purpose whose journey was all the more compelling for its detours.

Teresa's spicy, messy, and meandering spiritual journey cast my own struggles in a new light. Perhaps the discontent that had dogged me for the past year was not a spiritual dead end or a signal that I needed to work harder at tidying up my life. Maybe it was the opening chapter in a love story like the one Teresa had lived, a story in which a divine protagonist pursues his beloved with reckless ardor and ultimately wins her heart. Reading about Teresa's ecstatic prayer experiences—in which she felt Jesus consuming her with a love so sweet and piercing that she thought she might die on the spot—I felt a desire for divine intimacy kindled within me.

I also felt inspired by the discovery that Teresa's ardent faith had not squelched her natural boldness and originality but purified and intensified both, allowing her to use her gifts for a higher good. For Teresa, faith was a source of liberation, not oppression. She surely was a product of her times; her apologies for "womanly dullness of mind" make that clear. Yet Teresa defended a woman's calling to the same heights of mystical prayer to which God calls men and praised women for the special love and faith they showed Jesus while he was on earth. In an early draft of *The Way of Perfection,* she laments that the all-male ranks of judges in her day see "no virtue in women that they do not hold suspect," and she looks forward to the day "when everyone will be known for what he is . . . these are times in which it would be wrong to undervalue virtuous and strong souls, even though they are women." Slapping the feminist label on Teresa may be a stretch, but this trailblazer's single-minded focus on God's will led her to embark on adventures and undertake risks that would have intimidated most men of her day—and most secular feminists of ours. Through it all, Teresa retained her Spanish wit and zest for life, encouraging her nuns to join her for laughter, music, and dancing during recreation periods and delivering spiritual insights in an earthy, intuitive voice that reveals a uniquely feminine spiritual perspective.

Meeting Teresa marked a significant step in my nascent

spiritual journey, though I did not understand its full significance until years later. Teresa was the first woman saint I discovered as an adult; she was the first to model a mixture of faith, femininity, and freedom that I could admire and appropriate for my own life. I had no plans to join the cloistered Carmelites and no illusions that my mumbled daily prayers would morph into ecstasies anytime soon. It did not cross my mind that I should forgo plunging necklines or an extra beer on my girls' nights out, much less don a hair shirt or maintain monastic silence.

For all the differences between Teresa's life and mine, though, I could see strong parallels: an aching hunger for meaning, boredom with worldly pleasures and success, a passionate and often prideful intensity that could be used for great good or great folly. In Teresa, I saw the kind of woman I might become if I ever took God seriously enough to try. And I found a friend to whom I could turn in prayer, someone who could give Jesus an extra nudge on my behalf when I needed help overcoming the temptations of superficiality and sensuality that Teresa knew well.

## A Way Forward

The immediate upshot of my encounter with Teresa was a change in my New Year's Eve plans. Ever since we parted ways for Christmas break, my boyfriend had been making daily long-distance calls from his home in Boston to convince me to join him there for the holiday. I thought it sounded fun at first, but the more absorbed I became in Teresa's story, the less the trip appealed. I knew that it would be an occasion of temptation, as his plan entailed me staying at his house, and I knew that he saw my visit as a way to cement our status as a serious couple. He recently had started quizzing me about his various postgraduation career options to see if I considered them lucrative enough to make him a good husband and provider. His affection was genuine, and I could tell that he had big plans for us. My cross-country trek would signal that I shared those plans.

The more I listened to my heart, and to God's voice speaking in it, the more I realized that I did not want to make long-term plans with a man who regarded God as a competitor for my loyalties and faith as something best kept on the margins of life. I had taken up with such men before, and I knew I would be tempted to do so again. Here and now, though, I had a choice: I could continue clutching this man as a placeholder until I found someone or something more satisfying, or I could surrender the relationship and take a chance on God instead.

I decided not to go to Boston for New Year's. And three days after I returned to campus in January, I broke up with my boyfriend. I offered a lame excuse about needing to spend more time with my friends because I was too cowardly to give the real reason, lest word get out that I had become a religious fanatic. I knew that on a Catholic college campus like mine, having a little faith was commendable. But having too much—the sort that led you to dump perfectly good boyfriends, spend your lunch breaks at noon Mass, or take controversial church teachings too seriously—was a recipe for social isolation or at least ridicule. Better to be labeled shallow, stuck-up, drunk, or debauched—anything but devout.

After the breakup, my life did not change overnight. In fact, anyone watching from afar that semester would have noticed little change at all. I became more diligent about attending daily Mass and carving out time for daily prayer and spiritual reading, but I kept those habits hidden from even my closest friends. It had not yet occurred to me to return to the sacrament of confession. And though I felt a shaky sense of peace taking root in my heart, whatever was happening inside me was still not strong enough to curb my vanity and vices. It just made me enjoy them less.

Even the breakup brought me little comfort. I had assumed that my bold if badly executed act of obedience to God's will would result in a shower of blessings. Instead, I received some devastating family news shortly afterward that left me reeling with sadness and missing my boyfriend, who had since taken up with another coed, who looked like a shorter, skinnier version of me. I spent the rest of my final semester occupied by a down-to-the-wire job hunt that collided with my overloaded class schedule to make the spring unusually stressful.

After four years of doing whatever I wanted, I finally was trying to follow God's lead. And things seemed to be getting worse, not better. Reading Teresa's writings and tales from her life, as I did voraciously that semester, I felt a pang of painful recognition when I came across a story of the sick and exhausted reformer traveling to one of her besieged convents amid a fierce rainstorm. Her horse-drawn cart hit a pothole, and Teresa hit the mud headfirst. "Lord, if this is how you treat your friends," she quipped to Jesus, "no wonder you have so few!"

My awkward first attempts at resuscitating my relationship with God were not entirely fruitless. I later would come to see them as baby steps that helped me get my bearings before I tackled a host of more complicated problems relating to love and freedom, marriage and motherhood, the mystery of suffering, and my role as a twenty-first-century woman in a two-thousand-year-old church. My search for answers would span fifteen years, take me to places I never imagined I would go, and force me to reconsider nearly everything I thought I knew about what it means to be a liberated woman. It would be years before I recognized my efforts as a quest to understand my feminine identity in light of my Christian faith and contemporary feminism, to grasp the essence of what Blessed Pope John Paul II called the "feminine genius." Still, something important already had happened by the end of my college years: I had learned that the very saints I once considered irrelevant to my search could prove indispensable guides.

Teresa was the first. Although I still had no answers to most of the questions I had asked on that windowsill eighteen months earlier, Teresa's example convinced me that my journey to understand who I was and how I should live as a woman was inextricably bound with my journey toward God. Seeing her transformation from a party girl who chased pleasure and status with abandon to a saint who marshaled her prodigious talents and energy for service to God, I felt hopeful that my own natural intensity could find a nobler outlet than barhopping and résumé building. Teresa's squandered youth and stumbles on the path to sanctity reminded me that no matter how much time I had wasted in starting my interior journey, it's never too late to take the first step.

2

# A Child Again

The call came on a bleak January night in 1996, shortly after I returned to Milwaukee for my last semester of college. I was sitting at the desk in my bedroom, facing a mound of reading material for my eighteen-credit course load and a pile of résumés that I still needed to send out.

Mom was on the line. She had taken my father to see the doctor about his forgetfulness, and the news was not good. He had Alzheimer's.

I tightened my grip on the phone and stared at the bare white walls of my bedroom as I absorbed her words. My eyes fell on the Celtic cross that Dad had brought me from Ireland a few months earlier. I wanted to believe the promise it symbolized, to cling to the hope I heard in Dad's voice when he came on the line and told me, "Everything will work out." But as I hung up, I felt only numbness, then emptiness and dread.

Sitting there in the stillness, I tried to imagine what the coming years would bring. A long-buried memory suddenly sprang to mind. It was an image of me as a little girl, bundled in blankets and whispering prayers to Jesus before I fell asleep. Two petitions concerning Dad always made the list: I wanted him to live long enough to walk me down the aisle on my wedding day, and I wanted him to die of an illness that would give us time to say good-bye.

Those requests may seem morbid for a girl whose father was the picture of vitality during her childhood. Brimming with the energy of a man half his age and a passion for all things outdoors, Dad would burst into the house each weekday after work, toss his briefcase onto the table, and change his clothes in a flash. Then he would round up my older brother, Tom, and me and take us for bike rides, basketball games, or backyard tutorials on our fastballs and soccer kicks.

Dad was so young at heart that I never thought about his age until second grade, when a ponytailed soccer teammate asked me if the man cheering me from the sidelines was my grandfather. I always had known Dad was older than Mom—my parents often joked about their eleven-year age gap—but until then I had not pondered the novelty of having a father who was forty-five years old the day I was born. Did Dad's age mean that he would not live to see me grow into an adult? That he would die some random weekday morning, without warning or even a hug to bid me farewell?

I began to worry about heart attacks and strokes, to listen closely when I heard stories of men my father's age dropping dead in the middle of racquetball games and morning jogs. When my third-grade teacher launched a lesson plan on nicotine, I dutifully memorized each frightening fact and returned home to make daily presentations to Dad about the perils of pipe smoking. Impressed by my tenacity and guilt-ridden by my pleas, he soon quit.

During adolescence, after my brother left for college on a football scholarship and I found myself the sole focus of Dad's parental attention at home, my fears about losing him receded and his age began to bother me for other reasons. Too alike for our own good, we bickered frequently and our daily interactions were marked by irritation, most of it mine. Dad would shuttle me to school at a creeping pace no matter how late I was, constantly experimenting with new routes in what was, I was sure, an attempt to drive me insane. We quarreled as I teased and sprayed my hair in the passenger seat, and Dad moaned about the aerosol suffocating him, rolling his window up and down for effect.

In those years, Dad seemed so annoying, so embarrassing, so old. He had an argumentative streak as wide as mine and often looked and acted behind the times, with his big-band-era music, his wide-collared, 1970s-style shirts that he refused to retire, and his constant quips that had amused me as a girl but grated on me as a teen. I felt guilty when I met the fathers of my friends and found myself wishing Dad was more like them—younger, richer, less religious, more hip. I wanted to be gracious when Dad would reach out to me in the old ways—offering to take me for a bike ride or ski trip or ice cream run—but our outings often ended in stony silence. He wanted to relate to me as a daddy to his little girl.

I was no longer a little girl, though, and neither of us knew any other way to connect.

The tension between us subsided when I went to college, mostly because we saw so little of each other. As a high school senior in Colorado, I chose a college eleven hundred miles away. My visits home were infrequent, even after Dad's new job led my parents back to his hometown of St. Louis near the end of my freshman year. Dad frequently offered to make the six-hour drive to Milwaukee to see me, but I usually found excuses to put him off. Spending a weekend with Dad meant missing a weekend with my friends, and that was a trade-off I was unwilling to make.

Remembrances of those rejected invitations came flooding back to me that grim winter night, as I marveled that God might be answering my childhood prayers in some odd and terrifying way. I knew enough to understand the objective facts about Alzheimer's disease: It is a progressive, degenerative brain syndrome that causes memory loss, personality changes, disorientation, and death, often over a period of a decade or more. What I did not know—and had no desire to learn—was the subjective truth about dementia: how it feels to watch someone you love slowly surrender his independence, his memories, his mind.

My blissful ignorance did not last long. A few months after Dad's diagnosis, my parents traveled to Milwaukee to attend my induction into Alpha Sigma Nu, the Jesuit honor society. I had tried to convince them not to come—it really isn't a big deal, I said—but they were too proud to stay away.

The visit was tense. Mom spent it anxiously covering for Dad's memory lapses, and I spent it fighting to suppress irritation at his constant repetition of the same stories and his uncharacteristic bouts of peevishness. By Sunday afternoon, as I was walking my parents to their car, I was eagerly anticipating their departure. It would be good to get away from them, I thought, good to let Dad's troubles slip out of sight and out of mind again. I had troubles enough of my own.

Just then, I looked over and saw Dad grinning at me with a wild look in his eye.

"I'll race you," he said.

"What?"

"I'll race you, to the car. C'mon."

"I don't want to race, Dad. We're in the middle of campus."

"What are you, scared?"

I looked to Mom for help, but she only flashed a strained smile and nodded.

"Go on, Colleen," she said. "He wants to race."

"But I don't want to race."

"She's scared, Mary," Dad called out in a singsong voice that sounded like a child's.

"I'm not scared," I snapped. "I just don't want to run through campus looking like a two-year-old."

I could see Dad growing giddy, his blue eyes twinkling with mischief. Sixty-six years old and he wanted to race.

I looked over my left shoulder, then my right. Seeing no one coming, I sighed. There was no getting out of this.

"Okay," I said.

Dad clapped with delight, then crouched down on the sidewalk as if on blocks. His wrinkled fingers steadied him on the pavement. "Mary, you count."

I shot one more desperate look at Mom, who pretended not to notice my irritation. Heaving another exasperated sigh, I crouched down next to my father.

"All right you two," Mom began. "On the count of three: one, two—"

"Three!" Dad yelled as he struggled to his feet.

He barreled ahead, his stocky frame bucking the wind. I stood behind, bewildered, until Mom gave me a push.

"Go!" she whispered.

So I began to run. I was angry, confused, and embarrassed all at once, and right about the time I decided to start running hard, Dad hit the ground in front of me.

"Ow!" he yelped as he rolled on the concrete, clutching his left knee.

Mom ran to him, but Dad brushed her away. Seeing him there, lying sprawled on his back in the middle of the sidewalk, I felt a lump rising in my throat. I realized that this is how it would be; this is how Dad would grow old and die. It would not be the sudden good-bye I had feared. It would be something stranger and more tragic, a reversal I had never imagined.

All my life, I had been the child and he the adult. Now that I was finally old enough to know my father as an adult, he would become a child.

## "The Saint We Need"

I did not initially connect my grief over Dad's diagnosis to my nascent spiritual journey. I was content to bury my sorrow beneath anxiety about my job hunt and, later, preparations for a move to Memphis, where I had accepted a reporting position with the *Memphis Commercial Appeal.* As graduation neared, I continued my spiritual-reading regimen but made no effort to choose books that would help me cope with Dad's condition. I was more interested in finding another spunky, worldly-wise woman of faith like Teresa—someone I could relate to.

Teresa's most famous spiritual daughter in the Carmelite tradition happened to be one of my father's favorite saints: Thérèse of Lisieux. Dad always had described Thérèse as a sort of sleepy spiritual dynamo, a woman whose towering strength and wisdom were obscured by the plaster-of-Paris image painted by some of her devotees. For my part, I never could muster much interest in Thérèse. I was put off by her flowery quotes and her syrupy-sweet likeness on those rose-bedecked holy cards that seemed to turn up in the corner of every musty church. She looked like a bore.

Catholic activist Dorothy Day was another story. Dorothy's name was a familiar one in social-justice circles at Marquette, where her personal papers are archived, and in my own home, where my social-worker mother kept copies of Dorothy's penny publication, *The Catholic Worker,* on our coffee table. For years I read Dorothy's writings on the dignity of the poor and the necessity of Christian community. They had inspired me to volunteer at Milwaukee's Catholic Worker house. So I was intrigued when, a few weeks before graduation, I stumbled on Dorothy's biography of Thérèse.

At first glance, the two women could not have been more different. Dorothy was a journalist and suffragist who embraced elements of anarchism and socialism as a young woman, indulged in drinking binges at a Greenwich Village tavern known as the Hell Hole, and pursued various love affairs through her twenties, including a starter marriage that ended after a year. She aborted her first child and lived in a common-law marriage with the father of her second. When she was thirty, the birth of her daughter and a growing spiritual hunger led Dorothy to convert to Catholicism, a move that alienated her child's atheist father. This single mother then channeled her activist impulses into the Depression-era founding of the Catholic Worker movement, a collection of independent lay communities organized to offer hospitality to the destitute and marginalized. An ardent pacifist who blended traditional Catholic piety with a radical vision of social reform, Dorothy remained an outspoken advocate for workers, the homeless, and the poor for the remainder of her eighty-three years. In 2000, some two decades after her death, John Paul named Dorothy a "Servant of God," the first step in the Catholic Church's canonization process.

The subject of Dorothy's 1960 monograph, *Therese,* had led a much less exciting life, at least on the outside. In contrast to Dorothy's peripatetic childhood and bohemian youth, Thérèse enjoyed a bourgeois upbringing and spent all her life in the same quiet corner of northern France. A nineteenth-century cloistered Carmelite nun, Thérèse died of tuberculosis at age twenty-four, just five weeks before Dorothy was born. She founded no communities, engaged in no missionary work, and left no legacy of social activism. She was unknown outside the walls of her convent. Even within those walls, her fellow nuns fretted as she lay dying that they would have a tough time composing an obituary, since she had never done anything noteworthy.

When Dorothy first read Thérèse's autobiography as a new convert, she agreed. The plainspoken journalist dismissed Thérèse's *Story of a Soul* as "pious pap." Some three decades later, though, Dorothy had reconsidered, finding Thérèse captivating enough to devote a full-length biography to the saint. She had come to see Thérèse as "the saint we need," one whose childlike simplicity and love of God made her uniquely suited to challenge the hopelessness and powerlessness that modern believers feel when confronted with life's trials and the world's ills. In a technological society obsessed with rationality, efficiency, and productivity, Dorothy said, Thérèse is a reminder that the human person's highest calling is love: "She speaks to our condition. Is the atom a small thing? And yet what havoc it has wrought. Is her little way a small contribution to the life of the spirit? It has all the power of the spirit of Christianity behind it. It is an explosive force that can transform our lives and the life of the world, once put into effect."

Dorothy's endorsement made me take a second look at Thérèse, first by reading Dorothy's biography of her and later by reading Thérèse's own letters and account of her life. As I learned more about Thérèse, I came to share Dorothy's appreciation for this childlike saint and to see how she could help me make sense of what was happening to my father.

## The Little Way

The story of Marie Françoise Thérèse Martin begins in 1873 with her birth to Louis and Zélie Martin, devout Christians who have been declared "blessed" by the church and are, themselves, one step away from canonization. Thérèse lost her mother to breast cancer at age four and was doted on by her widowed father and four older sisters, all of whom eventually became nuns. She was deeply spiritual as a girl but also headstrong and hypersensitive, prone to pout over a stray comment that upset her or a trifling pleasure denied her. At thirteen, a Christmas Eve conversion led her to renounce her coddled ways. Less than two years later, after lobbying everyone from her father and the local bishop to Pope Leo XIII himself, Thérèse obtained special permission at age fifteen to enter the Carmelite community in Lisieux to which two of her older sisters already belonged.

Sister Thérèse of the Child Jesus and the Holy Face spent nine years in Carmel. Her rapid progress in intimacy with God during that time went largely unnoticed by her fellow nuns. That was no accident. Thérèse cultivated a spirituality based on hidden acts of love and sacrifice.

Although she admired such great saints as Joan of Arc and Teresa of Ávila, Thérèse felt incapable of imitating their bold feats and demanding penances. She sought a spiritual path more suited to her weakness and imperfections, one she described as "very straight, very short and totally new." As Thérèse explains in *Story of a Soul*:

> We are living now in an age of inventions, and we no longer have to take the trouble of climbing stairs, for, in the homes of the rich, an elevator has replaced these very successfully. I wanted to find an elevator which would raise me to Jesus, for I am too small to climb the rough stairway of perfection. I searched, then, in the Scriptures for some sign of this elevator, the object of my desires, and I read these words coming from the mouth of eternal wisdom: "*Whoever is a LITTLE ONE, let him come to me*" [Prov. 9:4]. And so I succeeded. I felt I had found what I was looking for. But wanting to know, O my God, what you would do to *the very little one* who answered your call, I continued my search and this is what I discovered: "*As one whom a mother caresses, so will I comfort*

> *you; you shall be carried at the breasts, and upon the knees they shall caress you"* [Isa. 66:13, 12]. Ah! Never did words more tender and more melodious come to give joy to my soul. The elevator which must raise me to heaven is your arms, O Jesus! And for this I had no need to grow up, but rather I had to remain *little* and become this more and more.

Thérèse's "little way of spiritual childhood," as it came to be known, grew out of Jesus's command in the Gospel of Matthew: "Let the little children come to me, and do not hinder them, for the kingdom of heaven belongs to such as these" (Matt. 19:14). Such scripture passages convinced Thérèse that what Jesus most wants from his followers is not great deeds but great love, an interior attitude of total, childlike confidence in God. "I see that it is enough to realize one's nothingness, and give oneself wholly, like a child, into the arms of the good God," Thérèse writes. "Leaving to great souls, great minds, the fine books I cannot understand, I rejoice to be little because 'only children, and those who are like them, will be admitted to the heavenly banquet.'"

Thérèse believed that the surest way to cultivate and express this childlike abandonment to God was to offer him small, everyday acts of love: going out of her way to befriend the crankiest nun in the convent, refusing to complain when accused of a misdeed she didn't commit, choosing to cheerfully and silently endure a frigid bedroom or pointed insult or another nun's habit of splashing dirty water on her when they did the laundry together. Thérèse offered up these slights and sufferings as flowers strewn before the throne of her heavenly father. "This is how my life will be consumed," Thérèse writes, ". . . strewing flowers, that is, not allowing one little sacrifice to escape, not one look, one word, profiting by all the smallest things and doing them through love."

Thérèse's little way was not about telling herself or God that such irritations didn't bother her or faking feelings she didn't have. Her sensitive nature was precisely what made her acts of kindness and patience a sacrifice. And despite the girlish language she employed, Thérèse braved intense physical and spiritual suffering in the last years of her life, resolutely offering her sorrows back to God with love as she lay dying.

After her death, Thérèse quickly became one of the church's most beloved and renowned saints. Theologians have spent more than a century unpacking the depth and originality of her spiritual insights; the basilica dedicated to her in Lisieux draws more than 2 million pilgrims a year; and her autobiography, written at the request of her prioress sister, became a worldwide best-seller. Called "the greatest saint of modern times" by Pope Pius X, Thérèse was canonized a mere twenty-eight years after she died. In 1997, a century after her death, John Paul declared her a Doctor of the Church—the youngest in church history and one of only four women who have been so honored. He praised Thérèse's focus on loving and serving God in the mundane circumstances of daily life, a focus he saw as inextricably entwined with her nature as a woman. "In approaching the Gospel," John Paul said, Thérèse "knew how to grasp its hidden wealth with that practicality and deep resonance of life and wisdom which belong to the feminine genius."

## A Father "Crowned with Glory"

One of the most ingenious features of Thérèse's spirituality was how it allowed her to deal with what she called her father's "great trial": his descent into dementia.

Like me, Thérèse knew the agony of watching a bright and beloved parent gradually lose touch with the world around him. Louis Martin's troubles started shortly after Thérèse entered the convent, with a series of paralytic strokes that left him progressively more confused and disoriented. Over a span of six years, he endured hallucinations, memory lapses, slurred speech, increasing dependence on the relatives who cared for him, and even confinement in a mental institution.

Thérèse's cloistered lifestyle did not allow her to see her father more than a handful of times after she entered the convent. She remained acutely aware of his suffering, however, and wept privately over his condition. In her autobiography, she describes how she felt upon learning of his move to the psychiatric hospital. After years of asking God for the privilege of suffering more for the sake of Christ, Thérèse felt overwhelmed with sorrow. Yet she saw meaning in this "most bitter and most humiliating of all chalices." She writes: "Ah! That day I didn't say I was able to suffer more! Words cannot express our anguish, and I'm not going to attempt to describe it. One day, in heaven, we shall love talking to one another about our *glorious* trials; don't we already feel happy for having suffered them? Yes, Papa's three years of martyrdom appear to me as the most lovable, the most fruitful of my life; I wouldn't exchange them for all the ecstasies and revelations of the saints."

Thérèse's unusual reaction to such awful news intrigued me. Even more intriguing was the way she viewed her father's increasing dependence as an avenue to greater intimacy with his loved ones and God. Once a robust man and daily communicant known for his cheerfulness, Louis had started suffering bouts of weeping and taken to covering his head with his handkerchief. He continued to manifest joy amid his pain and personality changes, however, speaking frequently of heaven and reminding his daughters to pray not for his cure but that God's will be done. Even his stay in the psychiatric hospital became an occasion of grace, as Louis labored to inspire other patients, share his food with them, and grow more accustomed to taking orders than giving them. Thérèse noticed her father losing interest in earthly things and saw God "flooding him with consolations" even as Louis lost his status and possessions—a purification process she believed God was allowing to make her father more like the suffering Christ. Louis agreed. "I know why God has sent me this trial," he said. "I never had any humiliation in my life; I needed one."

Louis's humiliation reached its pinnacle during his last visit to Thérèse and her sisters at the convent. He had to be wheeled in to see them, and despite his struggles to communicate, he could not manage to speak to the "little queen" with whom he once engaged in so many spirited conversations. As he was being wheeled away, a crumpled and childlike Louis raised his eyes and pointed up, managing two last words for his beloved daughters: "In heaven."

For Thérèse, her father's trial ended not in tragedy but in triumph—union with God after a long process of becoming the kind of childlike follower that Jesus extols in the Gospels. She believed that all of Louis's losses and humiliations had refined his soul and made him someone to be admired, not pitied. "Now that he is in heaven," Thérèse writes, ". . . never again will the divine hand be removed from the head it has crowned with glory."

## Signs of Decline

Reading those words from a saint my age, whose father had suffered the same fate that awaited mine, I felt a powerful bond with Thérèse. Part of that connection came from parallels I saw between Thérèse's personality and my own: her desire to do great things for God, coupled with a painful awareness that most heroic feats and harsh penances were beyond her reach; her intense sensitivity, which made her both empathetic and thin-skinned; and her natural impatience with irritating coworkers and companions, an obstacle to holiness that she had transformed into an opportunity for showing Jesus her love. Thérèse was no notorious sinner, but she had conquered the sort of deep-seated, everyday shortcomings that I saw impeding my own spiritual growth. And she had done so through a faith based on love, not mere duty, guilt, or fear.

Perhaps most important, I identified with Thérèse's tender and trying relationship with her father. The childlike affection she felt for him, mingled with her excruciating adult understanding of how much he was suffering, resonated with me. I sensed steel beneath Thérèse's sweetness—the strength of a woman wise beyond her years who refused to avert her gaze from her father's trial or deny the faith that told her that trial had eternal merit. Seeing dementia through Thérèse's eyes gave me a new perspective on my father's illness. And the more I reflected on Thérèse's life and wisdom, the more I felt drawn to spending time with Dad.

I found plenty of opportunities after graduation. A year after I moved to Memphis for my first newspaper job, I was offered a reporting position at the *St. Louis Post-Dispatch*. I happily accepted. My entire immediate family lived in St. Louis by that point—my brother had followed my parents there shortly after his college graduation to pursue a sales career—and it seemed like the right place to be, at least for a few years. I was grateful for the chance to jump to a larger newspaper while moving closer to Dad in his time of need.

Dad was delighted to have me near. An old-time Democrat with a passion for his historically liberal hometown daily, he reveled in my front-page articles and, later, my editorials in the *Post-Dispatch*. What's more, he loved seeing me so often. After a long day in the newsroom, I would swing by my parents' south St. Louis apartment for a visit. Dad would clap his hands at the sight of me, clasp me in a bear hug, then invite me to sit down and tell him what was new in my life. He frequently forgot my answer, but I enjoyed our conversations anyway.

Dad's chipper attitude made it easy to overlook his limitations, at least during short visits. Longer visits were another matter. I learned that in December 1999, when I traveled to Ireland with my parents. All of us had been there before: My father had visited with his own parents decades earlier; my parents had toured there together in 1995; and I had taken my maiden voyage with a college friend in 1998. I planned this trip for the three of us because I wanted to drink in those rugged seaside vistas and enjoy the hospitality of our Irish cousins again, this time with my Irish father at my side. I knew it would be my last chance to see the Emerald Isle through his eyes.

I planned the trip meticulously, careful to include visits with relatives on the east, south, and west sides of the island. I plotted stops at all the must-see attractions that Dad had described to me as a child, including the hauntingly beautiful Galway Bay, which my father's mother grew up glimpsing from her tiny farmhouse window. Dad used to sing me to sleep with the words of Arthur Colahan's melancholic tune "Galway Bay":

*If you ever go across the sea to Ireland,*
*Then maybe at the closing of your day,*
*You will sit and watch the moon rise over Claddagh*
*And watch the sun go down on Galway Bay. . . .*

*And if there's going to be a life hereafter,*
*And somehow I am sure there's going to be,*
*I will ask God to let me make my heaven*
*In that dear land across the Irish Sea.*

When we caught our first glimpse of Galway Bay midway through our trip, I pulled our rental car to the left side of the road and hopped out, eager to take it in with Dad. Mom raved at the sight, but Dad barely could be persuaded to get out of the car. He acted the same way at most of the other sights: tired, cranky, confused about why we were there, and anxious to move on.

It was odd behavior from a man whose best friend once theorized that his rear was made of leather, for all the driving he did. Dad had been known all his life as a consummate traveler, a road warrior who thought nothing of taking continent-spanning car trips for the chance to see just one more natural wonder or far-flung friend. His famous wanderlust, combined with the variable nature of his work in the nonprofit world, had led him to move our family to half a dozen states in the course of his career. To hear him bellyache now about a two-hour car ride along a stretch of scenery that he had described to me in breathless terms for the better part of twenty-five years was baffling, irritating—and painful.

I understood, at least in theory, that Alzheimer's accounted for Dad's sudden simulation of an incurious curmudgeon. I could tell that the unfamiliar surroundings, disruption of routine, and lingering effects of jet lag were taking a toll on my sixty-nine-year-old father, a toll that I naïvely had failed to anticipate when planning our whirlwind weeklong trip. Still, Dad looked as ruddy-cheeked and physically robust as ever. He walked with the same confident, unhurried gait; gripped the passenger-side grab handle with the same ferocious intensity when he disapproved of my speeding or sharp turns; and punctuated his stories with the same shopworn one-liners I had heard since childhood. The bizarre disconnect between Dad's old familiar habits and his odd new behavior left me alternately aggravated and confused. I kept expecting my father to be the same man I had grown up with, but he was changing before my eyes.

Dad's cousins noticed the changes, too. Although he delighted in seeing them, Dad could not remember their names or how they were related to him or what they had said to him moments earlier. The man who had once dominated social gatherings with his quick wit and elaborate stories now sat slouched in his chair, piping up only occasionally to offer a quip that made marginal sense. At the end of our visits, relatives who had assured Mom four years earlier that they saw no sign of Dad's memory problems now gave us knowing looks and sympathetic smiles.

In the bed-and-breakfast inns where we stayed, I could hear my erstwhile night-owl father snoring from all the way down the hall just minutes after he ducked into his room, often as early as 7 P.M. In the mornings, I watched my mother do the behind-the-scenes care I had not known about before. She would lay out his underwear, socks, pants, and shirt, find his glasses and shoes, guide him to the breakfast nook, nudge him not to use the silverware of the person seated next to him, and remind him to pour his coffee into a mug, not a cereal bowl.

The degree of Dad's dependence shocked and frightened me. My frustration gradually gave way to sorrow as I realized that I finally was seeing the decline that my briefer visits with Dad back home had disguised. By the end of the trip, I found myself alone in a chilly hotel room, scribbling tear-stained notes in my journal as I tried to make sense of what I had witnessed that week:

> I knew Dad has Alzheimer's. I thought I even knew his limitations. But it's never hit me so hard as it has in these past few days how helpless he has become and how much he, and I, have lost. I feel like I should be noticing what everyone else does: that Dad can talk; that he can laugh; that he makes sense (at least some of the time); that he still knows me. But I keep seeing—and feeling—the emptiness of a father who cannot communicate with me. A father who asks me relentlessly about my life but can't absorb my answer. A father who keeps slipping further and further into the past, before my existence, where I don't even matter. A father who is only half-there, half-cognizant, half-aware, half-sane. A glass half-full may be better than nothing. But it's no substitute for the real thing—my father, my real father, the one who sometimes forgot my age or my friends' names but never found himself incapable of talking to me

about something important or helping me think through a problem.

My father's decline accelerated after we returned to St. Louis. He went from getting lost behind the wheel to getting lost on his own block. I watched with heartache as the gifted wordsmith whose passion for writing had ignited my own now struggled to sign my birthday cards and the once-voracious reader of treatises on mystical prayer toiled to make sense of children's books about the saints.

After devoting his career to defending the vulnerable—through advocacy for the mentally handicapped, ministry to the sick and dying, and support for Catholic families in crisis—Dad now knew that vulnerability from the inside. My father always had told my brother and me that he loved us not for what we did but for who we were, that just being ourselves, with or without our accomplishments, was enough to make us great in his eyes. Now his condition was challenging me to return that unconditional love, to look beyond Dad's disabilities and see the blessing he still could be in my life.

## A Blessing Revealed

Reading Thérèse, and praying for her intercession, made it easier. I began to understand why she had been one of Dad's favorite saints, why a man who felt such passion for protecting the child-like felt such kinship with "the Little Flower," as he called her. As the youngest of five children born to working-class Irish immigrants in north St. Louis, Dad had learned early that love for God demands care for the vulnerable—like the hobos my grandmother fed from her porch during the Depression and the indigent hospital patients Dad served at the end of his career. Thérèse's little way of confidence and love made intuitive sense to a man who valued people more than things and trusted God's plans more than his own.

Even my father's faults made Thérèse and him a good match. Dad had struggled all his life with a volatile temper and what the saints sometimes call "intellectual pride." He was brilliant and courageous but not adept at picking his battles. He wanted to fight them all. He protected the weak with passion but had no patience for snobs, poseurs, or people he saw taking advantage of the defenseless. He often judged himself and others harshly.

In spite of those struggles—or, perhaps, because of them—Dad always reminded me of the same truth that echoes throughout Thérèse's writings: that God loves us no matter what mistakes we make, and our confidence in his providence should be boundless. Dad's own confidence in God sprouted from prayer. I first learned that as a girl, when I would rise before dawn, tiptoe barefoot through my toy-strewn bedroom and the darkened hallway, and find him in his office, reading scripture or praying in silence. Spotting me at the door, he would grin and wave me inside. I would scurry toward him, my blue eyes still filled with sleep and tousled auburn curls popping out in every direction as I hopped onto his lap with a mangled baby doll in tow. I would pour out my hopes and dreams, nightmares and worries. He would listen, then tell me about the heavenly father I could count on to care for all my needs. "Remember," he would say, quoting a favorite verse from Saint Paul's Letter to the Romans, "everything works together for good for those who love God."

Those memories took on new poignancy as I watched Dad navigate life with Alzheimer's and began to see evidence of the same transformation in him that Thérèse had seen in her own father. The signs were subtle at first: keener sensitivity to the suffering of others, more comments about God's love and less about others' faults, a greater humility that allowed him to accept help with gratitude more often than pique.

The most obvious sign of Dad's deepening intimacy with God was his irrepressible joy. Every day seemed to mark a new loss for Dad—another name he could not remember, another task he could not perform, another door of his mind shut forever as the disease invaded his brain. Yet Alzheimer's could not steal Dad's joy. Cultivated through a lifetime of putting people before possessions, principle before prestige, and love of God before all else, Dad's joy seemed to spring from some inexhaustible source, from a place the plaques and tangles of Alzheimer's could not reach.

Dad's joy was noticed by everyone he met, from his hairdresser, whom he serenaded with Irish songs, to the aides at the adult day-care center that he started attending a few years after we returned from Ireland. Dad would provoke smiles as he sauntered through the center, offering courtly bows and tips of an imaginary hat to the elderly women who stared at him from their wheelchairs. "Great to see you," he would say to his fellow dementia sufferers. "You're the best."

Led into a room full of patients in varying degrees of confusion, Dad would find his way to the corner where the most distressed one among them was muttering incoherently. Plopping down beside her, he would whisper, "We're all in God's hands," and stroke her arm until she grew quiet and calm. "I like to take care of people," he would tell me, when he could remember what he had just done.

The more dependent Dad became, the more his joy and confidence in God grew. His talk turned increasingly to eternal life, and heaven became a staple of his conversations. He still flashed his familiar temper at times, but those times sprang more often from fear or confusion than from anger. As his intellectual acuity faded, his insight into the spiritual crux of matters grew more penetrating than ever.

The relevance of Dad's insights often startled me. One Saturday afternoon I took a break from the hectic pace of my career and social life to pop in on Dad. I wanted to see him, but I wanted to be elsewhere, too: catching up on work, making plans for that night, staying in the loop with my twenty-something single friends. I was feeling antsy about settling in for another slow-paced, repetitive conversation with my demented father, just as I felt antsy about making time for prayer that day, which I had yet to do.

I ran up the back stairs of my parents' apartment at breakneck pace and snuck one last guilty glance at my watch as I barreled through the kitchen toward the living room, where I knew I would find Dad. Breathing deeply as I stepped into the room, I tried to exorcise that jittery feeling in the pit of my stomach that told me I did not have time for this visit.

Dad was sitting in his La-Z-Boy, looking unusually serious and serene. He beamed when he saw me, then clasped his fingers together and leaned forward to tell me what he had pondered that day.

"I'm not being scrupulous," he began, "and I'm not being pious. But it just came to me that I've been busy with all of these other things—work, running around, going here and there. But what is the really important thing?"

He paused for effect.

"It's God," he said. "I've realized that I need to focus on God, on spiritual things. It just came to me as I was sitting here."

I felt too taken aback to respond. Dad's words were exactly what I needed to hear that frantic, distracted day. We wound up chatting and laughing for the better part of two hours, my anxiety melting into the deep calm that Dad seemed to impart by osmosis whenever I allowed myself to enjoy him on his terms.

Sometimes Dad's spiritual encouragement came in even simpler forms: an unbidden "I love you" that reminded me of God's enduring presence after another disappointing date with Mr. Wrong, the gentle patting of his hand on mine when he sensed that I was stressed about a work problem he could not comprehend, an out-of-the-blue exhortation to keep my chin up on a day that I had managed to convince everyone else that I felt great. Sane people could not see through my fake smiles or detect the truth behind the feigned peppiness of my voice, but Dad could.

"Hang in there," he would tell me when I called to say hello after a particularly rough day. "You're in God's hands."

I asked Dad once what that meant, to be "in God's hands."

"It means we can trust God. We're in good shape," he said.

Such familiar phrases had rolled off me when Dad repeated them throughout my childhood. Now I found myself listening intently to Dad's words, struck by their potency coming from a man who had lost so much yet retained such faith. I started to see Dad in a new light, as a sort of spiritual beacon whose inability to comprehend the details of my daily life—or, for that matter, his own—had freed him to focus on eternal truths. I still pulled away from my parents' home frustrated and near tears some days, gunning the engine on the highway as I tried to outrun the image of my rumpled and confused father wandering dazed through a home that he no longer seemed to know. Other days, I dawdled in my apartment for hours before finally rousing myself to visit Dad or take him for a drive that loomed like a chore. Yet it often took no more than a few minutes after I plopped into the recliner beside him or buckled him into the passenger seat of my car for the tension to drain out of my back and neck, my impatience eclipsed by Dad's contagious delight in our time together. I typically left those visits with a surprising lightness in my chest and the conviction that in seeing my vulnerable and childlike father, I had glimpsed God's love in the flesh.

Dad's lost memories and abilities still pained me. I grieved for the father I could no longer converse with in the usual way, the once-eloquent man I saw yearning to connect with me yet unable to articulate his thoughts clearly. I feared what the coming years would bring, as Dad's dementia worsened and isolated him even more from those he loved.

Still, I could not ignore the blessings hidden in Dad's trial. It had become, in some strange way, a means of healing for the two of us. Dad's dementia—and, more important, his daily decision to lean on God in the midst of dementia—was showing me the character of a man I had taken for granted for too long. His growth in humility and his dependence on my help was drawing us closer together, leading us out of the rut our relationship had fallen into during my teen years. Although I recoiled at the thought of losing my father at a time when most of my friends still could take theirs for granted, I realized that in some ways I was more fortunate than they, because I had the privilege of watching my father respond heroically to what could have been a soul-crushing trial. God was making my father a better man before my eyes. And as he had with Thérèse, God was giving me a front-row seat to watch it happen.

## New Patroness

By January 2001, the five-year anniversary of his Alzheimer's diagnosis, Dad's childlike confidence in God had become a kind of touchstone for me. I had come to recognize his view of reality as more lucid than my own. I might remember what day it was or where I had put my wallet, but when it came to what really mattered, I was less enlightened than Dad. On most days, I still operated under the illusion that I was in control, that everything depended on my cleverness, my diligence, my merits. Dad knew better. He lived the truth of Jesus's words in the Gospel of Matthew:

> Look at the birds of the air: They neither sow nor reap nor gather into barns, and yet your heavenly father feeds them. Are you not of more value than they? And which of you by being anxious can add a single hour to his span of life? . . . Therefore do not be anxious, saying, "What shall we eat?" or "What shall we drink?" or "What shall we wear?" For the Gentiles seek after all these things, and your heavenly father knows that you need them all. But seek first the kingdom of God and his righteousness, and all these things will be added to you.
>
> *Matt. 6:26–27, 31–33*

Through a lifetime of seeking first God's kingdom and through his patient acceptance of dementia, Dad had cultivated the pure-hearted faith that Jesus described. He had become for me an image of spiritual childhood, a living model of Thérèse's little way. In my father's small, sometimes mangled acts of love—the rosaries he said daily for my intentions in the Eucharistic adoration chapel, even when he forgot what those intentions were, and the flowers he gleefully brought my mother, picked fresh from an unsuspecting neighbor's garden—I recognized the truth of Thérèse's signature insight: namely, that Jesus cares more about the love we put into our acts than the acts themselves. I finally understood what Saint Paul meant when he told the Corinthians, "But God chose what is foolish in the world to shame the wise; God chose what is weak in the world to shame the strong; God chose what is low and despised in the world, things that are not, to reduce to nothing things that are, so that no one might boast in the presence of God" (1 Cor. 1:27–29).

I realized that God was using my father's apparent weakness and foolishness to show me the childlike faith he wanted me to learn. And he was offering me opportunities to practice the hidden acts of love that Thérèse extolled.

In the years after I first encountered Thérèse, I began paying more attention to the way I interacted with Dad: the gentleness of my touch when I helped him with his jacket, the softness in my voice when I answered a question he had asked dozens of times, the eye contact I gave him at a crowded dinner table when he was getting lost in a fast-moving conversation. My natural haste and impatience often made even these little acts of attentiveness difficult to perform with love. Yet the more effort I made—to listen carefully to stories that once bored me or to treat Dad affectionately in public, even when his odd behavior caused a scene—the more I noticed the difference that effort made for me as well as Dad. I found myself rushing less, laughing more, and entering a state of peace around my father that I can only compare to prayer.

My discovery of Thérèse and her little way not only changed the way I looked at Dad; it changed how I looked at millions of others like him: the demented and disabled, the infirm and frail elderly, and the unborn. If what I was reading in the Gospels, learning from Thérèse, and seeing in Dad was true, then our culture has it exactly backward when treating such people as expendable. If productivity, efficiency, and rationality are not the ways God gauges a human person's value, then they are not the ways I should measure it, either. If childlike dependence on God is the mark of a great soul, then there are great souls hidden in all sorts of places where the world sees only disability, decay, and despair.

One spring afternoon I glimpsed in microcosm how Dad's disease had changed my perspective. My parents and I were riding together on a float in St. Louis's annual Hibernian parade, a festive and splendidly disorganized affair that overtakes the city's Dogtown neighborhood every March 17. Like the city's Mardi Gras parade, the Saint Patrick's Day parade features revelers on floats tossing sparkling plastic beads into a raucous crowd. Police officially forbid the throwing of beads—float dwellers are told to hand them out instead—but when the authorities are not looking, the beads fly.

As our float passed into the thick of the crowd, we were besieged with demands for the green, gold, and purple strands that we clutched by the dozens. Dad, sitting beside me wearing a patched Irish cap and a huge grin, delighted in the happy chaos. But the crowd's pleas confused him.

"Beads! Beads!" the crowd cried.

"Steve! Steve!" Dad answered, before leaning over to confide in a low voice: "I don't know who this Steve guy is."

I explained that they wanted our beads, not Steve. So Dad picked up a strand of purple ones, twirled them above his head like a lasso, and threw them—straight to the feet of a police officer.

The cop graciously gave Dad a pass. Not wanting to press our luck, I hopped off the slow-moving float to deliver my own beads. As I did, I found myself repeatedly drawn to people on the edges of the crowd who looked slightly out of sorts: a man with Down syndrome, getting shoved aside by drunken strangers; an elderly woman with a cane, straining to see from her lawn chair; a Vietnam veteran with scraggly hair haunting the periphery alone; three little girls dressed in threadbare sweatshirts that barely passed for green; a pair of dour-looking teenagers in black trench coats trying to get in on the action without looking like they cared. To each, I ran and hand-delivered beads, relishing the surprise in their eyes when they saw me passing up dozens of more boisterous, beautiful revelers for them. I wondered as we reached the end of the parade route: Why had I done that? It was a little thing, of course, but something I probably would not have thought to do a few years earlier. What had changed? I glanced over at my father, looking a little disoriented as he struggled to descend the float without falling, and suddenly knew the answer. Those outsiders and least ones, in all their forms, reminded me of Dad.

My growing awareness of God's exceptional love for the

vulnerable and marginalized had more consequential effects in my life, as well. Thérèse's emphasis on the "little ones" of the world—her insistence that we regard them not as burdens or embarrassments but as conduits of grace—transformed my worldview and my work. It is the reason I converted from vaguely pro-choice to passionately pro-life, the reason I began to take an interest in bioethics and end-of-life issues, and the reason I started writing in defense of people like my father, people who deserve to be protected and loved no matter what their abilities.

I adopted Thérèse as patroness of my writing career, discreetly placing a photo of her beside my computer at work and stopping by her statue during daily visits to my neighborhood parish. Kneeling before an image of the saint I once considered too childish to merit my attention, I prayed for a share of her maturity and strength. And I asked Thérèse to watch over my father, whose beauty of soul I knew she, of all people, could help me see.

3

# Trust Fall

In the spring of 2001, five years after I moved to St. Louis, I fell in love.

I was on a yearlong leave from my newspaper job at the time, working from my south St. Louis apartment on a book that would be published in 2002 as *The New Faithful: Why Young Adults Are Embracing Christian Orthodoxy.* The project was a labor of love and a young writer's dream. Thanks to a $50,000 journalism fellowship that I had recently won from the Washington, DC–based Phillips Foundation, I had the freedom to spend a year traveling the country, interviewing hundreds of my peers about what was then a little-noticed trend: the attraction of a growing number of young Americans to a theologically orthodox, morally demanding Christian faith. My interest in the trend stemmed from personal experience as well as professional observation, and I relished the chance to probe the spiritual hunger of my generation in such depth. I also enjoyed meeting so many fascinating young adults. And none fascinated me more than John.

I knew it was love almost immediately, within weeks of meeting him at a local conference for Christian medical students. Neither of us was seeking romance at the time. Having sworn off dating for a six-month stretch after an especially unsatisfying relationship, I walked into the bland ballroom of the St. Louis Airport Marriott that March morning seeking interviewees for my book. John came seeking ideas for integrating his studies at Washington University School of Medicine with his Christian faith, which he recently had reclaimed after a ten-year detour through atheism. A classmate of his introduced us, and I invited John to join an impromptu group interview I was conducting at the back of the ballroom. I wanted to hear from these top-flight students about their experiences reconciling religion and science in medical school.

The other interviewees responded to my questions mostly by bemoaning the biases of their secular medical professors and the evils of evolutionary theory. John offered more expansive, nuanced answers that left me wanting to hear more. It did not hurt that he had twinkling, slightly mischievous blue-green eyes, a dashing smile, and a knack for making me laugh. So when he accepted my request for a follow-up interview only on the condition that we talk over dinner at a romantic Italian eatery, I happily obliged. I brought my tape recorder and notepad, but a few glasses of wine and hours of conversation later, it was clear that we were in the middle of not an interview but a date—and a pretty wonderful one at that.

I had met hundreds of bright, talented, faithful young men and women while researching my book that year, but never anyone like John. He was all of those things and more: warm, curious, lighthearted, and utterly lacking in artifice. He was the sort of person who pauses to think before he speaks and actually means it when he says he'd rather talk about you than him. His love for Jesus was accompanied by keen understanding, from personal experience, of what it's like to feel distant from God and dissatisfied by superficial pieties.

It seemed that ever since John and I first began talking over toasted ravioli and Chardonnay that spring night, we had not stopped. Aside from my research trips and John's study marathons, we spent every free moment together. We could not say enough, learn enough, or see enough of each other. The more we said and learned and saw, the more we felt called to marry.

I had my doubts, however. Our blossoming romance ran afoul of several of my rules regarding love and work. The first: Never date a source. The second: Never date a man whose career ambitions could torpedo your own.

I had convinced myself that the first rule did not apply to John, since he never actually granted me a real interview. But the second definitely did, given that John recently had started medical school in St. Louis while I was counting down the months until I could finish my book and leave flyover country behind. I could tell from John's hectic medical school schedule that his free time as a physician would be scarce. Marrying him would mean giving up any feminist fantasies of sprinting down the career fast track while my husband stayed home to play Mr. Mom. It would mean that my children probably would not have the sort of omnipresent father I had enjoyed, one who could slip out of work regularly to pick them up from school and boast perfect attendance at their ball games and piano concerts. Especially worrisome for me as a writer on the cusp of publishing my first book, marrying John might mean shoehorning myself into the role of the dutiful doctor's wife and losing my own identity in the process.

Like most women in my generation, I had heard enough horror stories about feminist workaholics to know that I did not want to sacrifice my personal life at the altar of an all-consuming career. I had heard even more warnings about the other sort of sacrifice: the surrender of professional success that women are prone to make in fits of passion or panic over their biological clocks, only to wind up dependent on unappreciative men. As someone who had drafted her first résumé in sixth grade and had clutched it as a security blanket ever since, I found the specter of such surrender terrifying. I believed in work-life balance, but I always made my decisions with that order in mind: work, then life.

My growing intimacy with John threatened to change that. I could feel our love shifting the balance of my priorities, leaving me unsteady as I pondered our future. My anxiety about our competing careers mounted. One sweltering July Fourth afternoon, while we were munching on gyros together under the Gateway Arch, it bubbled over.

"I don't intend to be just a stay-at-home mom," I announced to John, apropos of nothing. "I won't just get stuck with a bunch of babies and not work. My career is important to me."

He nodded, staring at me as he struggled to get a grip on the shredded lettuce spilling out of his pita.

"I know a lot of doctors' wives do that," I continued. "They give up their careers; they focus on keeping house and raising kids. That's fine for them, but that's not me. That will never be me. I intend to keep writing, even after I have kids."

John nodded again. "I know," he said, between bites. "I love that about you."

His acquiescence rankled me. Maybe I was not being forceful enough.

"I serve God through my work, too, you know," I said, wiping my brow as I felt my face growing hotter. "I don't intend to give it up just to get married. If you're looking for a conventional doctor's wife, you're going to have to find someone else!"

I chugged my water and watched John warily.

"Well?" I asked between gulps. "What do you think?"

"I think your writing career is terrific. If I wanted a wife who had nothing to do but focus on me, I would never have been so attracted to you."

He paused, a smile spreading across his face.

"I want *you*," he said. "I love *you*."

Although I could feel my defiance melting, I pushed on, reminding him that we had grown up seeing different models of marriage. In John's family, his physician father worked outside the home while his dietician mother stayed home to raise their four children. She embraced her maternal and household duties with gusto, running a home where the monogrammed hand towels always matched, the tops of the chandeliers that no one could see were cleaned as thoroughly as the spotless kitchen counters, and dishes were cleared and washed minutes after you finished your last bite of mouthwatering, made-from-scratch apple pie. I admired her enthusiasm and aptitude for all things domestic, but I shared neither.

Maybe that had something to do with my mother, who had exhausted her inner domestic goddess long before her wedding day. As the oldest girl among twelve children, she spent her childhood changing diapers, scrubbing floors, and polishing shoes and silver and anything else my perfectionist grandmother saw in need of a shine. By the time she had a family of her own, Mom could muster little interest in housework beyond the basics. She earned her master's degree in social work while my brother and I attended elementary school, lugging her mammoth textbooks to the playground so she could study while we twirled on the monkey bars. She worked outside the home through much of my childhood, due largely to financial necessity, and split the cooking, carpooling, grocery shopping, and child care with my dad.

I knew that both our parents had made choices that suited their situations, so the models were tough to compare. What I did not know was which one John and I would follow. He would earn enough money to allow me to stay home with our children—something I recognized as a blessing—and the flexible nature of my career made working from home a realistic possibility. Yet even a flexible career requires time and strategic moves to flourish. Could I invest those things in writing while married to someone in a field as all-consuming as medicine? And what about where we lived? St. Louis was fine for now, but if I wanted to pursue my dreams of political and opinion writing, I figured I soon would need to move east to DC or New York.

John listened as I unloaded, then unpacked my concerns. He assured me that he was open to leaving St. Louis after medical school. He suggested that we hire a part-time nanny to help me once we had children so I could work from home. As for his career, he said he would choose a lower-paying medical specialty if it meant a higher-quality family life.

"It will work out," John said, reaching for my hand. "We'll make it work."

## An Unexpected Offer

For the next year and a half, we did. I finished my book in late 2001 and returned to my *St. Louis Post-Dispatch* job, content to continue my newspaper work until *The New Faithful* made its debut and I figured out what I wanted to do next. In May 2002, at the summit of a stunning sunset hike in Missouri's Ozarks, John officially proposed. We set a wedding date for the following summer.

Elated at the prospect of marrying John and no longer willing to leave St. Louis until he was free to leave with me in 2005, I began mulling prospects for a career move that would allow me to stay in town while he finished medical school. I ruled out staying at the newspaper; the daily grind of news reporting no longer held my interest, and even my move to the paper's editorial board a few years earlier had left me dissatisfied. There was never enough time or space to delve deeply into subjects, nowhere near as much as I had enjoyed while writing my book. The only newspaper position that still appealed was that of op-ed columnist, a coveted perch that would allow me complete freedom to choose my topics and write from my own point of view rather than that of the newspaper, while potentially reaching a national audience. But I saw no such opening anywhere on the horizon at the *Post-Dispatch*. Longing for more independent, intellectually fulfilling work and seeing no publications in St. Louis that would allow me to satisfy that longing, I lit on a new idea: the pursuit of doctoral studies in philosophy at Saint Louis University.

It was an unconventional choice for a young journalist but one that allowed me to indulge the intellectual interests I had neglected as an overscheduled, career-focused undergraduate. The program would take five years to complete. That time commitment intimidated me, especially since I did not plan to parlay the degree into an academic career like most doctoral students. I did not quite know what I would do with the Ph.D. after I earned it.

I enrolled anyway, figuring the extra time in St. Louis might work out well for other reasons—namely, Dad and his dementia. His condition was declining, and I knew the day was rapidly approaching when he no longer would be able to join me for the regular walks and talks that we now enjoyed. In a few years, he might not even recognize me. Why not stick around town a little longer, so John could finish not only medical school but also his postgraduate, three-year medical residency in St. Louis while I spent more quality time with Dad? Although I did not relish the delay in pursuing my big-city ambitions, graduate school would give me something productive and prestigious to do while I waited. My status as a doctoral student served as tangible proof, to myself as much as anyone else, that I was doing what I always liked to do when it came to my career: make a smart move that looked as good on my résumé as it felt in real life.

I left my newspaper job in June 2002, spent July attending World Youth Day in Toronto and a three-week seminar on Catholic social teaching in Poland, then launched my graduate studies in August. My book hit stores in September. To my surprise and delight, *The New Faithful* struck a nerve. I was deluged with media interview requests and speaking engagements that made it tough to focus on my more esoteric philosophy studies. Among the most intriguing offers I received was from a special assistant to President George W. Bush. He invited me to present my research on youth and religion to staffers at the White House.

I accepted, and John accompanied me to Washington for the trip. After spending an action-packed October week zigzagging with him from one DC speech and book signing to another, I headed alone to 1600 Pennsylvania, where I needed to clear security to enter the luminous ivory complex. My host gave me a whirlwind tour of the West Wing, and in the process I met Bush's chief speechwriter and handed him a copy of *The New Faithful.*

It turned out to be a fateful move. When I returned to St. Louis a few days later, his deputy called to say that he had been impressed with my writing on issues of faith and values and wanted me to consider joining his team as one of six presidential speechwriters. If I got the job, I would work directly with Bush on major addresses and craft his rhetoric on such domestic-policy issues as the faith-based initiative, judicial appointments, education reform, and abortion—the very topics where my views aligned most closely with the president's.

The offer floored me, and though the timing could not have been worse for our wedding plans, John urged me to apply.

"You have to go for it," he said. "It's a once-in-a-lifetime opportunity."

I knew he was right. So I hastily cobbled together an application amid cramming for my philosophy exams, then waited weeks for a response. The answer came on a frosty evening in December, while John and I were attending daily Mass together near downtown St. Louis. I normally kept my cell phone off in church but had decided otherwise on this night, having been told to expect an important call.

I felt my hands go icy as I ducked out of the cozy chapel to answer the phone. The clipped voice on the other end told me the news that I thought I wanted to hear: I got the job, and they needed me to start right away.

Snapping my phone shut, I stood shivering in the unheated hallway and tried to process what had just happened. Was I really about to become a White House speechwriter, to join that elite club of scribes who choose the words spoken by the leader of the free world? How had I wound up with this honor? And why did it leave me feeling queasy?

It was not that I did not want the job. The prospect of working in the White House thrilled me. I could put my faith into action at the highest echelon of government, while earning a golden-ticket credential more suited to my career aspirations than a doctorate in philosophy. A move to DC would require me to postpone my wedding, though—possibly for two years or more, since John still had several years left in medical school and I did not want to begin a marriage living in separate cities. The postponement probably would put an end to my girlhood dreams of Dad escorting me down the aisle on my wedding day, not to mention my hopes of shepherding Dad through his daily trials in late-stage dementia.

I peered through an orange stained-glass window into the chapel I had just left. Spotting John's silhouette on a kneeler inside, I remembered the first time I had watched him pray, while sitting next to him in church on a radiant Easter Sunday morning shortly after we met. Although the pastor had called the congregation to prayer, many in the crowd, myself included, were still stealing looks around the sanctuary. John was not. Clasping his hands between his knees and bowing his head low, he had squinted his eyes shut and leaned his broad shoulders forward to shield himself from distractions. Something about his bearing in that moment had struck me as both strong and humble, and utterly sincere. I had seen my father assume that same posture dozens of times when he did not know his little girl was watching him pray. *This is a good man,* I had thought, feeling slightly dizzy at the revelation. *This is the sort of man I've been waiting for.*

I knew then that I had found someone special, someone I did not want to leave. Now here I was, bracing for a cross-country move that would transplant me to a city known for goading its residents into trading personal happiness for professional success. I had no idea when I would return or when John and I would marry. Inhaling deeply, I swung open the chapel door and prepared to take my place by John's side, to whisper the news that suddenly seemed less happy than sad.

For the first time in my life, I felt sorry for my success.

## An Unlikely Guide

If I had decided that night to seek a saint who could help me reconcile my desire for a prestigious career with my yearning to marry, Maria Faustina Kowalska would not have been my first choice. Or my second. The mousy-looking, barely literate nun never experienced either. And at first glance, it would seem that the struggles she faced in her convent in pre–World War II Poland had nothing to do with my own.

Born poor in 1905, Faustina—whose given name was Helena—spent most of her thirty-three years performing menial chores. As a child she labored on her large Catholic family's farm; in her teen years she worked as a housekeeper to help support her parents; in the convent she washed dishes, peeled potatoes, pulled weeds, scrubbed toilets, and tended the door. Her only written work was a diary largely composed of words dictated to her. Unlike that of the fiery Teresa of Ávila or the charming Thérèse of Lisieux, Faustina's life story features no preconversion tales of a worldly youth or indulgent childhood. She was pious practically from birth. The closest she came to rejecting God was her decision to attend a dance as a teenager. Faustina briefly lost herself in the frivolity of the moment only to see a vision of the crucified Christ beside her on the dance floor, asking how much longer she would ignore his call to the convent. She packed her bag that night.

Devout as she was, Faustina did not coast to sanctity. Poor, sickly, and possessed of only a third-grade education, the aspiring nun was not a particularly attractive prospect for a religious order and she met rejection at convent after convent. She finally found a home in the Congregation of the Sisters of Our Lady of Mercy shortly before her twentieth birthday in 1925. The order turned out to be more active and less strict than Faustina had hoped, and in her first year there she experienced intense desolation that biographers have described as a dark night of the soul.

Sister Maria Faustina of the Most Blessed Sacrament, as she became known in the convent, clung to her faith during that bleak time. Three years after it ended, she saw a vision of Jesus standing before her. His right hand was raised in blessing. His left hand pulled away a robe that revealed luminous rays of red and white streaming from his chest—symbols of the blood and water that spilled from his heart when he was pierced by a lance on the cross.

According to Faustina's diary, Jesus asked her to paint his image with this inscription beneath it: "Jesus, I trust in you."

Wary of being deceived by an experience that may not have come from God, Faustina confided the incredible vision to her superior and her spiritual director. They ordered her to work with an artist to paint the image. She began keeping a journal of the many mystical experiences that followed over the next seven years, before her death from tuberculosis in 1938. During one of those experiences, she heard an inner voice directing her to say a new prayer on the beads of her rosary, an explicitly Eucharistic litany focused on Christ's passion that would become known as the Divine Mercy chaplet. Together with the image of the merciful Jesus and Faustina's six-volume journal, the chaplet formed the basis of the Divine Mercy devotion that has become one of the most popular in the Catholic Church today.

The message of that devotion is simple: The modern world, with its inhumanity and unbelief, needs God's mercy as never before. We cannot tap into that bottomless ocean of divine love unless we ask for it. Jesus desperately wants us to ask and to trust that we will receive. "The graces of my mercy are drawn by means of one vessel only, and that is trust," Jesus told Faustina, according to her diary. "The more a soul trusts, the more it will receive."

Among the first to discover and appreciate that message and the simple nun who relayed it was a young Polish seminarian named Karol Wojtyła. The future Pope John Paul II came across Faustina's writings while living in Nazi-occupied Poland during World War II. Convinced of the timeliness of her message in a world gone mad with war, he took up Faustina's cause as his own, promoting the Divine Mercy devotion as he ascended through the ranks of the church hierarchy. The scripture verse he repeated throughout his pontificate—"Be not afraid!"—reflected his desire to spread trust in God's providence as Faustina had. Her writings profoundly influenced his 1980 papal encyclical, *Rich in Mercy*, and John Paul canonized Faustina on the Sunday after Easter in 2000, declaring the day a new feast in the universal church dedicated to the mercy of God. In his last book, *Memory and Identity*, John Paul describes Faustina as "a particularly enlightened interpreter of the truth of Divine Mercy." She "was a simple, uneducated person," he writes, "and yet those who read the *Diary* of her revelations are astounded by the depth of her mystical experience."

## Faustina's Fruit

I was among those astounded by Faustina's depth, though it took me a while to appreciate her. First, I had to overcome my natural aversion to the fantastical elements of her life story—the tales of visions, locutions, and other supernatural phenomena.

It's not that I considered such things impossible. My Catholic faith taught me that Jesus could turn water into wine, rise from the dead, and make himself fully present—body, blood, soul, and divinity—in what appears to be nothing more than a tiny Communion wafer. Surely, if he wanted to appear to one of his followers to share a message about God's mercy, he had the power to do so.

Still, stories like the ones surrounding Faustina always made me skittish. They seemed over the top, even embarrassing, and I appreciated the fact that the church does not require Catholics to believe in such private revelations. Even approved ones such as Faustina's—the authenticity of which church officials originally doubted, then accepted—are a matter of individual judgment. They exist, as the *Catechism of the Catholic Church* says, not "to improve or complete Christ's definitive revelation, but to help live more fully by it in a certain period of history." In other words, Jesus is God's last word in terms of revelation; the rest is gravy.

Since I generally prefer to skip the gravy, I paid little attention to Faustina's doorstop of a diary when my mother gave me a copy after my college graduation. Five years later, while traveling for *The New Faithful* shortly after Faustina's canonization, I noticed the Divine Mercy image popping up in church after church. John Paul's endorsement of Faustina and her devotion piqued my interest, so I pulled out my rosary beads and taught myself the Divine Mercy chaplet. The chaplet—a Catholic prayer form that uses prayer beads—took far less time to recite than a rosary. I liked its explicitly Eucharistic overtones, and as I murmured its final refrains, a wave of peace washed over me. Something about the chaplet seemed special to me, and especially powerful.

That experience led me to crack open Faustina's journal. In reading her words and those she said Jesus dictated to her, I could not ignore how they spoke to my heart. More impressive to me than Faustina's visions and locutions was her trust in God. Faustina trusted quietly, steadfastly, and totally. She trusted amid intense physical suffering borne in silence, amid derision and slights from fellow nuns, amid the humiliation of hearing some to whom she confided her mystical experiences dismiss them as fabrications or evidence of mental illness. She seemed to embody that biblical proverb I had always loved: "Trust in the Lord with all your heart, and do not lean on your own understanding"

(Prov. 3:5). Faustina's elevation to the altars came later, but during her lifetime she leaned on God alone.

"I will hide from people's eyes whatever good I am able to do so that God himself may be my reward," Faustina writes in her diary, referring to her ministry of making secret sacrifices for the sake of sinners—including concealing her mystical gifts from those who considered her ignorant and useless. Faustina relied on God's providence, not worldly respect, to secure her future and that of the Divine Mercy devotion. As she explains, "I do not understand how it is possible not to trust in him who can do all things. With him, everything; without him, nothing. He is Lord. He will not allow those who have placed all their trust in him to be put to shame."

I saw the fruit of Faustina's trust firsthand when I traveled to Poland in July 2002. As I meandered through the cobblestone streets and cool, dark churches of Kraków's Old Town, the Divine Mercy image of Jesus confronted me at every turn. I saw replicas of the image tucked into taxi rearview mirrors, crammed into nooks and crannies of shops and restaurants, and posted in Eucharistic chapels where Poles of every age and income came to pray. I saw the image hanging over the altar in the five-thousand-seat Basilica of Divine Mercy, a shrine built on the outskirts of Kraków next to Faustina's convent. Two million pilgrims from around the world flock there each year to profess their trust in God and celebrate his mercy. The sight of them stirred me, and as I stood beneath the window of Faustina's humble convent cell, I marveled that this international movement to celebrate God's mercy began with one woman saying, "Jesus, I trust in you"—and meaning it.

Trust had never been my strong suit. Not in the spiritual life or any other part of life. A natural-born worrier never at a loss for new material, I liked to profess confidence in God but keep plan B in my back pocket in case God let me down. The same went for my human relationships. I protected myself and my interests, gave generously but only to a point, and always kept one eye on the exit. If nearly a dozen interstate moves and a decade of dating had taught me anything about relating to people, it was how to walk away.

My self-reliance and studied detachment had served me well throughout my peripatetic childhood and compartmentalized college years. They proved less helpful in the face of the work-life conflict that unfolded the night I won the White House job. Although I did not know it at the time, Faustina and her Divine Mercy devotion were just what I needed to guide me through that dilemma. Her spirituality of trust would become both an inspiration and a rebuke to me in the challenging days ahead.

## White House Life

I began my trek to Washington on January 1, 2003, in the middle of a New Year's Day blizzard. John devoted the final days of his winter break to loading my belongings into a rented Penske truck, hitching my eight-year-old Toyota Corolla to the back, and driving me fourteen hours to DC. With the help of some friends I knew in Washington, he moved me into a quaint-but-chilly little apartment off Connecticut Avenue. The next morning I gave him a lift to the airport so he could fly back to St. Louis to start his spring semester.

Our good-bye was tense and rushed. Exhausted from the move and stressed by our coming separation, we bickered as we snaked through the downtown DC traffic and across the Potomac. By the time I pulled off the George Washington Memorial Parkway into Reagan National Airport, we were locked in stony silence. I watched as John disappeared behind the sliding doors, then I sped away, eager to put some distance between us before my tears fell. I cried all the way back to my new home.

My first week in the White House was desolate. I had been told that I needed to start as soon as possible because the State of the Union address made January an especially busy time in the speechwriting office. After scrambling to get there, I spent my first day alone in a windowless office in the Eisenhower Executive Office Building, filling out paperwork for the FBI background check and wondering when my new boss would stop by to say hello. I passed the next four days pretty much the same way. No one introduced me at the first staff meeting, and when I asked what I should work on, I was told to wait for an assignment. It came at the end of that week. By the next Monday, I found myself line editing my first speech beside President Bush.

I had not been expecting to work with him that day. I knew that Bush was an early riser, but no one had told me that he expected his speechwriters to arrive before sunrise on the mornings after they had turned in remarks for his review. I felt faint when I strolled into my office at 8 A.M. and found "POTUS" listed on my caller ID. I had missed the president's call—twice—and he still was waiting to see me so we could discuss the speech I had written for him on education reform.

I arrived in the Oval Office minutes later, breathless and sporting my cheapest blazer, a lumpy, pea-green number I had picked up at T.J.Maxx for $13. My drab brown slacks drooped at the waist, and my still-damp hair hung limply around my puffy eyes. I had spent most of the night before lying awake, wondering if this move had been a mistake. Now sleep-deprived and still panting from my sprint through the West Wing, I tried to remind myself that it's an honor to work for a president even if he fires you the second week.

"Is this the education lady?" Bush barked at his secretary as I appeared in the doorway.

The president was sitting behind his desk, reading glasses on his nose and the pages of my speech spread before him. After his secretary told him I was the culprit, he gave me a quick once-over from his perch on the opposite side of the majestic room.

"I met your mom in St. Louis," he called to me, half-hollering.

My mother had told me she introduced herself to him on a rope line recently, but I did not expect him to remember. This seemed to be a good sign. Maybe he would not fire me after all?

"Here, have a seat," Bush said, gesturing to a chair on his right that faced his desk.

I sat down beside him, feeling like a tardy and slightly troublesome pupil called to the front of the classroom so the teacher can keep an eye on her. My boss sat to the president's left, looking nearly as tired and frazzled as I did. The president began to lead us on a forced march through my prose. Editing pen in hand, he proceeded paragraph by paragraph, explaining what he liked and what he didn't. *These lines here are bold, clear, and full of active verbs—that's good. That paragraph is redundant; why are we telling people the same thing we told them earlier in the speech?*

While the president spoke, a White House photographer hopped around the room snapping candids of us. I tried to focus on what Bush was saying while breathing in the history all around me—the famous Resolute Desk where little John John had played in the kneehole panel while John F. Kennedy worked; the venerable portraits of Abraham Lincoln and George Washington that I had seen in my history textbooks as a schoolgirl; the plaster ceiling medallion with the presidential seal that reflected off the sunbeam oval rug, making the room blindingly bright.

By the time we reached the end of the draft, I was relieved that Bush seemed fairly pleased with my work. Most of his complaints centered on jargon added to my original draft by various bureaucrats during the White House staffing process, a tedious exercise in editing by committee that presidential speechwriters famously abhor.

Working with the president was a thrill that first time and each time that followed. Meetings in the Oval Office or Roosevelt Room were particularly memorable, and as Bush saw more of me, he warmed up, making a point of letting me know when he especially liked my latest speech.

"*Cah*-leen," he would drawl, grinning at me as my cheeks flushed and every head turned my way, "great job today."

The president could be testy with staffers, but he usually treated me with a certain softness and good humor. Perhaps he sensed that I was more ink-stained wretch than savvy politico, someone too engrossed in the task at hand to be gathering gossip for a White House exposé. For my part, I saw Bush as a man of integrity, fallible but sincere in his faith and desire to do right by the American people.

Exhilarating as it was to write for the president, my workdays often were a slog. Everything was a struggle: extracting the policy details I needed to write a substantive first draft of a speech; prodding the various cabinet secretaries and their staffs to give me timely feedback; sidestepping intramural squabbles that dueling White House factions tried to settle in the pages of presidential speeches; and successfully blocking unhelpful edits without infuriating the powerful appointees and would-be wordsmiths who proffered them. I lost as many battles as I won and often found myself forced to defend to the president or his secretary a speech that contained lines I had known Bush would hate—lines I hated, too.

The process left me stressed and exhausted. It did not help that I was the president's only woman speechwriter. While other White House offices boasted more balanced gender ratios, the speechwriting shop remained an old-fashioned boys' club. I felt keenly the difference between my former job in a raucous newsroom full of feisty women writers and editors and my new office in which the only other women played supporting roles as researchers and secretaries. I quickly realized that women in the office were expected to speak only when spoken to—even if the man speaking to them was yelling—and watched with bemusement as male interns barely out of high school enjoyed more deferential treatment than full-time women staffers, including me. I learned to swallow hard before entering a room, steeling myself for the wisecracks and exaggerated expressions of annoyance that made me feel like a pigtailed tagalong invading the boys-only tree fort. I had never encountered such chauvinism on the job before, and I had no idea how to respond to it, other than keeping my head down, plowing through my day, and calling John at night to unload my woes.

## Waiting for a Sign

Although I looked forward all day to my conversations with John, they typically crackled with tension. He felt too exhausted after gruelling hours in the hospital to chat for long. I felt frustrated by the distance between us and his lack of answers to the questions I repeated each night: Should we reschedule the wedding? Should he move to DC? Should I come home? John's ability to quarantine those questions and focus on his work during the week grated on me, since I struggled to do the same. My heart was in St. Louis; my desire was for marriage; and I felt drained living as the single woman I no longer considered myself to be.

We took turns visiting each other each month, trying to pack four weeks' worth of face time into forty-eight hours. The result was more tension, exacerbated by the fact that both of us were sliding back into the stubborn single ways we had stretched beyond during our courtship. After regularly digging my car out during blizzards, wrangling with an irascible maintenance man to get emergency apartment repairs, and standing toe-to-toe with pushy politicos who tried to test the resolve of the novice speechwriter, I chafed at John's habit of arriving in town and taking charge: driving the car, choosing the restaurant, steering the conversation away from work when I had hours more venting to do. For his part, John bristled at my bossiness and tendency to ruminate on the problem of our separation rather than enjoy our brief time together.

We talked about reuniting all the time, of course. Our initial plan was for John to transfer to a medical school near me. We soon learned that no area schools were accepting transfer applications, save one with a second-rate reputation located more than an hour from DC. If John transferred there, he likely would lose course credits and graduate later with a diploma worth significantly less than one from Washington University, which had been rated the nation's most selective medical school the year he was admitted. Transferring schools also could handicap his chances of landing a spot in his first-choice residency program, which in turn could stymie his efforts to combine family-friendly hours with a family-supporting salary down the road.

John did not refuse to transfer, but as the spring application deadline neared, he showed little interest in proceeding. I reluctantly admitted to him and myself that he should drop the idea. That left only one option if we wanted to marry before John's graduation in two years: I would need to leave the White House.

The prospect both elated and terrified me. I relished the thought of returning home to marry John, of starting a family and a life together. I also liked the idea of seeing more of my parents again. Living just miles from them in St. Louis had made Dad's continual decline from Alzheimer's easier to bear. Now each of my visits from DC left me startled and saddened by how much he had lost since I had last seen him. I could not shake the sense that no matter how important my work in Washington, I was missing something more important back home: my final chance to enjoy leisurely moments with the father I saw fading fast.

For all my longings, though, I could not fathom how I would explain such a move to my colleagues and friends—or myself. *I'm leaving the White House to get married.* Merely mouthing the words mortified me, making me feel like one of those pitiable, pre-makeover characters slouching through the opening scene of a Lifetime TV movie. Leaving the White House, even if I wanted to go, could set a subservient tone for the rest of my life as a wife. I never had considered myself a fervent feminist, but I respected modern feminism's first commandment when it came to relationships: Never give up more for a man than he gives up for you.

I had practical concerns, too. What would I do for money if I moved back to St. Louis? John would not earn a paycheck for two more years, and I could not fathom returning to my old newspaper job or my abandoned graduate studies. Both felt like depressing steps backward after my celebrated departure for DC. Speechwriting had not turned out to be my dream job, but pursuing the career options that did inspire me—freelance writing and speaking, working for a Beltway think tank, penning my own op-ed column, or hosting my own talk show—surely would not be feasible in the Midwest, at least if I wanted to make enough money for John and me to live on. Even if there were a way to get paid doing those things from St. Louis, finding that way would take time. I felt overwhelmed just thinking about trying to find a new job while working at the White House, and I feared running afoul of an administration policy that banned outside job hunting while working for the president. I also feared leaving the White House so soon after I had arrived. Wouldn't my short tenure leave a black mark on my otherwise unblemished résumé?

I knew John wanted to marry soon, as I did. Each time I testily reminded him what a sacrifice I would be making if I left the White House, though, he curtly reminded me that I did not have to leave. We could wait to marry until after he graduated and began earning a salary; he could choose a residency program in DC; and I could stay at the White House as long as I liked.

John's refusal to sell me on St. Louis left me feeling more alone in a decision that I resented having to make. I started to stew about the injustice of it all, to sympathize for the first time with those anguished discussions of women's work/life dilemmas that I once had dismissed as feminist bellyaching. Why were women always the ones who had to fret about our ticking biological clocks and family obligations? What good was it to have so many career opportunities today if women still were the ones who had to make the steepest sacrifices for love and family?

I wanted to blame patriarchy for my conundrum, blame my job, blame John. Deep down, though, I knew something else was pulling me home. It was the force of my own desires, desires that sprang from a soft, passionate, feminine part of me that I thought I had smothered with résumés and credentials long ago. Decades of perfectionism and compulsive achievement had not managed to kill her off. Now she was daring me to reject the smart move and take a chance on love.

Fearful of heeding that voice and tired of trying to think my way out of this fix, I turned to prayer. One prayer in particular anchored me. It was the Divine Mercy chaplet. Brief and repetitive, it was perfect for those dark mornings when I arrived at the White House before sunrise, anxious about my ongoing dilemma and the day's coming storms. I would walk through the towering, empty halls of the Eisenhower Building, my clicking heels making a lonely echo off the ornate ceilings as I hurried to my office. Stepping inside, I would close my door, check my caller ID to make sure I had not missed an Oval Office summons, then settle into a couch that looked as old as George Washington himself and make the sign of the cross. After thumbing through my pocket Bible and briefly meditating on the psalms—the ones about waiting on the Lord for answers especially resonated—I would pull out my rosary and silently mouth these words as I moved my fingers through the beads:

> [On each of the five Our Father beads] Eternal father, I offer you the body and blood, soul and divinity of your dearly beloved son, our Lord Jesus Christ, in atonement for our sins and those of the whole world.
>
> [On each of the fifty Hail Mary beads] For the sake of his sorrowful passion, have mercy on us and on the whole world.

The chaplet's rhythmic, cross-focused refrains quieted the chattering in my head, allowing me to sink into stillness with God. I could feel my worries receding to the background as I worked my way through the prayer. I always ended by saying, "Jesus, I trust in you." The phrase comforted me, not because it was entirely true but because saying it made it seem more so.

Throughout the spring, as I pondered the pros and cons of leaving the White House, I continued this morning routine. I scoured scripture for answers, feeling comforted as I read, again and again, about God's providence in granting our deepest desires. Verses like those in Psalm 37 buoyed my spirits:

> *Trust in the Lord, and do good; so you will dwell in the land, and enjoy security.*
>
> *Take delight in the Lord, and he will give you the desires of your heart.*
>
> *Commit your way to the Lord; trust in him, and he will act.*
>
> *He will bring forth your vindication as the light, and your right as the noonday.*
>
> *Be still before the Lord, and wait patiently for him.*
>
> *Psalm 37:3–7a*

Each time I pored over such lines or murmured, "Jesus, I trust in you" at the end of my chaplet, I silently, tearfully, and sometimes angrily begged God to answer the desire of my heart. I asked him to show me a win-win move that could release me from my dilemma. If an escape from this difficult choice were not possible and my longing to return home came from God, I reasoned, then the least he could do was grant me a clear sign that I should act on that desire: a dynamite, unsolicited job offer in St. Louis that would make it easier to leave or an insurmountable problem in DC that would make it impossible to stay.

Neither came. Stasis prevailed, at work and with John, and the neon sign I demanded did not materialize. Morning after morning, I felt a strong sense of God's presence in my life and my heart but little clarity about what I should do. It was as if God, like John, was refusing to push me toward a choice lest I later resent him for forcing my hand.

Casting about for guidance and dispirited by my indecision, I found myself increasingly drawn to Faustina's message of blind trust in God. I could sympathize with the loneliness, abandonment, and uncertainty about the future that echoed through her writings, and I longed to translate those feelings into wholehearted dependence on God as she had. Reflecting on her life and words, I began to notice a connection that I had overlooked before: the link between trust and humility. It takes humility to assent to follow God even when he refuses to install floodlights on your path or tell you where it will lead. Faustina's trust was rooted in that sort of humility, a refreshingly uncommon virtue in the Beltway bubble I inhabited. Her refusal to demand answers from God or defend herself from detractors went against everything the world—and especially Washington—says about what it takes to be successful and secure. It was not that Faustina did not care about her future or her reputation. She simply cared more about imitating Jesus in all things, including the humiliation he suffered without complaint. As she writes, "Humiliation is my daily food. I understand that the bride must herself share in everything that is the groom's; and so his cloak of mockery must cover me, too. At those times when I suffer much, I try to remain silent, as I do not trust my tongue which, at such moments, is inclined to talk for itself, while its duty is to help me praise God for all the blessings and gifts which he has given me."

I always had fancied myself a contrarian who cares little for worldly opinion. Passages like that one reminded me that I harbored the same obsession with human respect that I resented in others. Nowhere was this more apparent than in my work. I fiercely guarded my professional achievements as the core of my identity, and my trust in Jesus rarely touched that realm. To leave the White House and return home to marry John would expose me to potential humiliation: People might see my decision as retrograde and foolish or proof of my failure to make it in the big leagues. To face that threat would take both trust and humility—virtues that I knew I did not, by nature, possess.

## A Subtle Shift

As the interminable drizzle of early spring gave way to balmy, flower-speckled days, I finally started to settle in at the White House. The long hours and conflictual nature of the work still weighed on me, but I was learning to navigate the system and enjoy myself more.

Ordinary workdays often brought once-in-a-lifetime experiences: riding in the president's motorcade to hear him deliver major addresses I had written; greeting him as his helicopter landed on the South Lawn or as he bellowed my name while marching to an East Room press conference; flipping through cable news channels and hearing snippets of my speeches played as pundits pronounced solemnly—and usually, wrongly—on the reasons Bush had spoken this or that "code word." I relished standing in the back during Rose Garden events and watching ordinary Americans whose stories I had woven into my speeches shed tears when they heard the president speak their names and acknowledge their struggles. I felt important when taking calls at home on Sunday mornings from Secretary of State Condoleezza Rice and at the office on Sunday nights from political guru Karl Rove. I delighted in inviting friends to join me for private tours of the West Wing and welcome ceremonies for heads of state, hosting my mother for Fourth of July fireworks with the first family, and laughing with John as he exchanged waves with a slightly annoyed President Bush in the Rose Garden after Barney, the first dog, scampered to John instead of his master.

Every time I stepped into the Oval Office or threaded my way through a gaggle of tourists and flashed my badge for admittance to the grand, gleaming White House complex, I marveled at God's mysterious ways that had brought me to this place. Still, it bothered me that my best days were those during which I was too immersed in the excitement of White House life to remember the life I had left behind in St. Louis. I worried that the longer I stayed, the more I would harden into someone who no longer found it difficult to work around the clock, jab elbows with irascible bureaucrats, and forgo the extended prayer time and heart-to-heart conversations with John that I once needed to get through the day.

I had expected that working in a Republican White House would introduce me to many other women who shared my concerns. That was not the case in my office, at least among the female interns clustered outside my door. Working with my door open one day, I heard one of them—a well-heeled Harvard student whose shoes and shawl cost more than I earned in a week—tell the story of a classmate who had become engaged while still in school and planned to make a postgraduate career of motherhood.

"She just wants to get married and have babies," the intern clucked, before lowering her voice to convey the dirty secret behind this woman's bizarre choice. "She's *Catholic*."

The gaggle of twenty-somethings encircling the intern shook their heads, mouths gaping in horror. Conflicted as I was about my own situation, I could not help commenting on this one.

"I'm Catholic," I said, flashing Ms. Harvard a wry smile as I strolled out into the midst of them. "And I'm engaged and want to get married and have babies. I think a lot of women want that."

Her eyes grew wide and she glanced around at her audience as if to plead for support.

"Well, yeah," she said. "But not right after college!"

"Why not?" I said. "It's a free country. That's the great thing about freedom. Different women can make different choices. I don't see anything wrong with hers."

I ambled past the group and out the door to noon Mass, sure that talk of my peculiar views would dominate the office lunch discussion that day. I wondered: Was my desire for marriage and motherhood merely an outgrowth of my Catholic faith? Or had my Catholic faith reawakened a desire intrinsic to my feminine nature, one the world had convinced me to suppress for too long? Had feminism changed things so much that a woman who earns a degree from Harvard before marrying at twenty-two is considered a pitiful throwback to the Dark Ages?

I tried to remember how I had felt about such things a decade earlier, during my own college days. I probably would have been one of those interns clucking with disapproval at the bride-to-be. Now I found myself envying her courage. Married at twenty-two! With a degree from Harvard—and no immediate plans to use it in the workforce! That takes chutzpah.

Every day in Washington—at the White House, on the Metro, in my upper-middle-class neighborhood in Northwest DC—I saw women who had made the opposite choice. Some had married late; many had not married at all. Some were mothers, but most were older than I hoped to be when I had children. They looked frazzled and frayed as they darted down the halls at work, barking orders on their cell phones while rushing to meetings and attempting to merge sixty-hour workweeks with motherhood. They panted as they chased their toddlers around playgrounds on the weekends, looking exhausted by a job that their young Latina nannies performed with ease during the week. Many had adopted children from overseas, a common practice in wealthy DC circles where women routinely waited until their forties to conceive and often found that even in vitro fertilization could not fulfill their desire for a biological child.

At twenty-nine, I still felt slightly unprepared for children, yet I knew that I should not wait much longer before starting a family. Staying on the Washington fast track for several more years probably would make it harder for me to get off that track when the time came for motherhood. If I really wanted to stay home with children while keeping a hand in the working world, I needed to start carving out that sort of flexible career path before I had children, not afterward.

My sense of urgency intensified when a twenty-seven-year-old, newlywed colleague of mine was diagnosed with colon cancer. A sharp and conscientious young woman with intense loyalty to Bush, she worked gruelling hours as our office's research director, often pulling all-nighters at her desk as she fact-checked important presidential addresses. When I asked her once how she liked married life, she told me that her husband had lamented her long hours at first but eventually quit complaining and took a job that left him as little free time as she had. Although she said it with a laugh, her story made me sad. She was a serious Catholic, and I sensed that she looked forward to the day when she could live a saner life and start a family. Unfortunately, that day never came for her. Her cancer spread quickly, and a few months after she was diagnosed, she was dead.

Her death shook me. She handled her trial with courage and grace, but I could not help wondering how I would feel if that diagnosis had hit me instead. All those hours we had logged at the White House looked good on a résumé and gave us the satisfaction of serving our country. In my colleague's case, they earned her a get-well bouquet of flowers from Bush himself—a gift that thrilled her. Yet I suspect she would have happily traded those flowers—along with all those overtime hours—for a few more days with the husband and parents she loved.

Perhaps I was projecting my own concerns onto her. I only knew that after three decades of driving myself from one achievement to the next, I felt a subtle shift taking place in my depths. Morning after morning, as I read my psalms, prayed my chaplet, and paid attention to such scenes unfolding all around me, I felt myself letting go—a little at first, then more and more. A lifetime of striving had brought me to the epicenter of worldly power. Now that I finally could direct my workaholic tendencies into the high-pressure, high-status job I always had dreamed of, my drive to strive had waned. God had replaced it with new yearnings: for union with John, for time with my father, for a personal life that no longer merely fit into the margins of my career.

The idea of fulfilling this desire still frightened me, however. For months I continued to vacillate and demur. Every time I tried to commit to leaving the White House, I pulled back, questioning myself and John about whether I was making the right call. I still lacked the unmistakable sign I wanted from God to convince me that leaving DC was his will, a decision he would bless.

One summer evening I was walking home from work up Connecticut Avenue, listening to the interior debate over my dilemma that played out in my brain every day around this time. I turned up the volume on my headphones, hoping that the old Alison Krauss CD that John and I had discovered together years earlier would drown out my anxious thoughts. They weren't getting me anywhere, anyway.

The song that came on next was one I had never noticed before. Krauss was singing about the lure of wealth and worldly security, professing that for all of life's ups and downs and unknowns, she would rather rest in God's hands than rely on her own plans. Her angelic voice made me want to breathe in her grace-based message. But I could barely hear it over the din of fears and worries still looping through my mind, reminding me that relying on Providence is something best done only after you hammer out the practical details. Just then, I heard these lyrics: *Faith can see right through the circumstance/Sees the forest in spite of the trees.*

Tears stung my eyes. That simple little refrain was not a neon sign. It wasn't a memo from God telling me what to do. It was, simply, an invitation.

All this time, I realized, God had not been asking me to obey him. He had been asking me to trust him. I could stay in DC or return to St. Louis. Either way, he would be with me. But going home was the desire he had put in my heart, and going home took more trust. It would take the sort of trust that Faustina had: that no-holds-barred, no-looking-back faith that allowed her to risk looking crazy for love of Jesus and made her a powerful conduit of his grace as a result. The only way to gain that trust was to act as if I already had it, to step out in faith with nothing other than God's hands to catch me if I fell.

I grinned as I felt the warm evening sun beat down on my skin. It was all I could do not to run the last few blocks to my apartment. I couldn't wait to call John. I couldn't wait to tell him—without any caveats or conditions this time—that I was coming home.

## Independence Day

I left Washington in late 2003, a little less than a year after I arrived. After some whirlwind planning, John and I had managed to arrange for a Christmas wedding that coincided nicely with his winter break. I had not found my next job or even looked; I decided to spend my remaining White House days doing the best work I could, then live on savings in St. Louis while I searched for my next opportunity.

Announcing my departure to my boss was not easy. Several other speechwriters had left in recent months, making me a veteran in the office.

"That's not good," he said, when I broke the news that I was going home to get married. "That's not good at all."

President Bush's response was more magnanimous. He sent me off with a memorable Oval Office good-bye; my boss said it was the longest departure ceremony he had ever witnessed. My mother flew in for the occasion, and the three of us stood laughing as the president leaned back on his desk and regaled us with stories of his adventures campaigning in St. Louis and his own nuptials with his wife, Laura. At one point Mom choked up while confiding her trials in caring for my father. Bush listened carefully.

"Those things test your faith," he said quietly.

Before leaving his office, I told the president that I was honored to have served as his speechwriter and sorry I could not stay. He nodded and looked at the floor, graciously refusing to notice the emotion crackling in my voice. Then he looked up and said brightly, "I have a wedding gift for you."

Bush began darting around the room, rooting first through the drawers in his desk and then through those of a nearby bureau, trying to find a presidential pin to give me. He held it aloft when he found it, presenting the small blue jewelry box to me with a proud smile. As we hugged and posed for our final photos, I tried to freeze the moment in my mind, knowing it probably would be the last time I saw this president or this room in person.

At the end of that week, after enjoying a hurried bit of farewell cake with colleagues, I closed the iron gates of the White House complex behind me for the last time. It was a perfectly crisp fall afternoon, and John had flown in to help load my belongings into another rented Penske truck, this time to take me home. I felt light-headed with happiness as I walked out to the elliptical driveway to meet him.

"I can't wait to spend the rest of my life with you," John said as we embraced.

"Me, too," I answered.

Cruising down Constitution Avenue a few minutes later, I took one last look at those gleaming white columns and grinned. John and I were holding hands and heading west, into the sun. We soon would be married. Never in my life had I felt so free.

I had not felt this free in my swinging-single days at Marquette, as a single-minded careerist in my early twenties, or in that year I spent traveling solo across America on my journalism fellowship. I thought I knew freedom each of those times, but the freedom I knew on this sun-dappled autumn afternoon was something else entirely. It was the kind of freedom that comes not from breaking rules or cutting ties but from making a commitment that costs you, and knowing that God will see you through. Sweeter and deeper than mere license, this liberty had eluded me all those years I spent protecting my own interests and making sure that I never gave more than I got. It was only in sacrificing something for love that I had found release. Now, finally, I felt ready to enter marriage with my heart wide open.

The decision to leave the White House might have been easy or inconsequential for someone else. For me, it was an arduous and invaluable form of marriage preparation. Wrestling through it forced me to reevaluate my priorities and learn the art of surrender, which I would need to practice again and again in married life. It pushed me to decide how much I would trust God to care for my needs in the coming years, as I gradually exchanged my independence as a single woman for interdependence as John's wife.

What Faustina had discovered in her convent cell halfway around the world, I had discovered, with her help, in the White House. The crucial question when it comes to faith is not "Do I trust God?" but "Is God trustworthy?" And the only way to answer it is by leaning into his merciful arms and letting go.

4

# A Mother at Heart

I always knew I wanted children. I just didn't want too many, too soon. And I didn't want the stress of trying to support them on the negative income of a medical student and an unemployed writer.

So when John and I returned from our honeymoon in January 2004, I reminded him that we must be very, very careful about avoiding pregnancy. We both respected the Catholic Church's teaching against contraception and agreed that we should use only natural means to postpone parenthood, and then only for a serious reason. We figured our precarious financial situation qualified, given that he was still a full-time student and I was coasting on savings and soon-to-expire medical benefits while mulling my next career move.

Our economic prospects brightened in September 2004, when I became a salaried, St. Louis–based fellow at a Washington, DC–based think tank. The position gave me the financial security, benefits, and Beltway standing I needed to pursue a full-time writing and speaking career from home. Meanwhile, John was within striking distance of graduation and would be earning a salary—albeit a medical intern's meager one—in only ten months.

Despite losing my main rationale for dodging motherhood, I still hesitated to pursue it. I worried that my irregular menstrual cycles and family history of fecundity might mean I was destined to follow in the footsteps of my grandmother. She had borne a dozen children while struggling to master the old-style rhythm method; she rolled her eyes whenever I asked about its effectiveness. My natural family planning instructors assured me that today's NFP methods were more reliable and that the larger families typical of NFP users were simply evidence of NFP's success in fostering openness to life. Although I believed them in theory, I still struggled to read my body's fertility signs and relied mostly on long bouts of abstinence to avoid pregnancy. I figured that as soon as I stopped being so careful, I would find myself in Grandma's shoes: pregnant or nursing for two decades straight, overwhelmed by more children than I could handle.

I knew that if John and I welcomed children as a gift, God would bless us. Even Grandma said as much. Which child, she used to ask me, would I give back? Still, I resented the fact that this new venture would demand more sacrifices from me than from John. When he began dropping hints about starting a family, I responded with reasons to wait. Perhaps we should postpone until I had established myself more on the national lecture circuit and as a pundit on the cable news shows where I recently had gained a foothold. Maybe we should wait until he had his first paycheck in hand, not just in sight; until we had ironed out our marital conflicts over the division of housework; until we had taken more trips to places we lacked the time and money to see as newlyweds.

One of those places was New Orleans. I had been there before, several times, but not with John. At the end of December 2004, after celebrating our first wedding anniversary in St. Louis, we hopped into the car and headed south to spend the remainder of John's winter break enjoying the City That Care Forgot. We booked into the Hyatt Regency next to the Superdome, ate a sumptuous New Year's Eve feast at Galatoire's in the French Quarter, rang in 2005 amid thousands of other revelers in Jackson Square, then devoured a half dozen beignets with the rest of the night owls at Café du Monde. We did everything we could not have done with a baby in tow.

The next morning we slept late, brunched at Brennan's, hopped onto a streetcar, and hopped off in the Garden District. After ambling for hours past elegant southern mansions, we wandered into a humbler neighborhood where we found ourselves confronted with the baroque beauty of Saint Mary's Assumption Church. We stepped into the grand old church and learned from a woman there about its most famous pastor, a nineteenth-century priest named Blessed Francis Xavier Seelos, who had died after contracting yellow fever from the victims he served. When she handed us his crucifix and urged us to pray with it, we settled into a pew together to figure out what we wanted to ask of God.

The answer that popped into my head surprised me. After

such a leisurely, lavish weekend, I could think of only one gift I wanted—the very gift that meant the end of such weekends. I wanted the love between John and me to bear fruit. I wanted to give myself totally to someone who needed me utterly. I wanted—

"I'd like to pray for a baby," John said, his eyes raised expectantly as he turned to search mine.

I caught my breath, then smiled.

"Me, too."

## A Black Hole

It seems fitting that John and I first prayed for a baby in pre-Katrina New Orleans. Like residents of that hurricane-ravaged city, we would look back on early 2005 as the calm before a terrible storm. By that fall, the church where we had prayed had suffered rain and wind damage, the Superdome environs where we had stayed had deteriorated into a war zone, and 80 percent of New Orleans was underwater. Meanwhile, seven hundred miles up the Mississippi River, John and I were reeling from our own natural disaster.

I was sitting on my bed when it struck, combing my hair in front of my dresser mirror and looking forward to a dinner date with John. He had just answered the phone in his office. I continued combing as I heard him jovially greet the doctor we had seen that week, a friendly colleague of his who had run some diagnostic tests on us to rule out major problems that might explain our failure to conceive after ten months. I stopped combing when I heard John's robust voice suddenly turn quiet and dull. I could make out only the rough contours of the conversation, but the upshot was clear. The doctor had discovered some sort of problem, maybe more than one, and his discovery had catapulted us from the large crop of normal couples that take slightly longer to conceive to that smaller, more pitiable pool dependent on medicine or miracles to achieve pregnancy.

As I overheard John drilling the doctor with questions, his voice falling lower after each excruciating pause, I stared at my face in the mirror. I felt as if I were someone else looking at my thirty-one-year-old body. I noticed for the first time the faint creases at the corners of my eyes and a laugh line on my left cheek. *Shouldn't have tanned so much in college,* I thought. *Shouldn't have wasted so much time before settling down.*

I robotically resumed combing my hair, my mind racing as I recalled the women I knew who had struggled with infertility. I thought of horror stories I had heard about humiliating and invasive procedures, exorbitant medical bills, heartbreaking miscarriages, and marriages strained to the breaking point. I remembered how many times I had murmured encouragement to such women while silently thinking, *Please, God, don't let that ever happen to me.* Now here I was, facing the same fate.

When I heard John hang up the phone, I waited a moment, then went to his half-open office door and peered in. He was sitting at his desk with his head in his hands. I rapped lightly as I entered. He did not move.

"Was that the doctor calling about the test results?" I asked.

"Yeah," he said, his head still in his hands.

"What'd he say?"

"They're not good."

"How bad?"

John slowly swiveled in his chair to face me. He looked ashen. "Pretty bad."

"Does he think we can get pregnant?"

"He said it doesn't look good."

I felt wobbly as the words hit me. I glanced at the yellow pad on John's desk where he had scrawled some notes, including ratios I could make out from where I stood. One said: "1 in 1,000." I stood frozen for a moment as I watched John turn back to his desk, resting his head again in his hands. Then I stepped forward and crouched beside him. John reached out to embrace me, his gaze still cast down as we leaned in to hug. We stayed that way—clutching each other in the silence—for what felt like forever, neither of us wanting to pull away and look at the other's crestfallen face.

The rest of the night was a blur. John and I trudged to our dinner date anyway, our conversation alternating between happy talk about the high error rates in medical tests, gallows humor about the fringe benefits of a child-free life, and long, heavy silences. He sank into a deep slumber shortly after we arrived home, but I lay awake for hours. Around midnight, I tiptoed out of bed and into the hallway. I paused at the door of the office we had hoped to turn into a nursery, then crept into the living room, where the beaming smiles of our wedding portrait seemed a cruel reproach. I felt as if every dream I had for our marriage and our life together had exploded. I knew that the doctor had left a little room for hope, but I dreaded the uncertainty and anguish that lay ahead. I sensed that infertility would be a harsher trial than any I had known, one for which my impatient personality made me particularly ill suited.

Kneeling on our worn, mint-green living room carpet, I folded my body into a ball with my forehead to the floor and my hands cupping my face. I wanted to be swallowed up, to disappear for a few years until someone could tell me how this story would end. Squinting my eyes shut, I tried to block out the waves of shock and grief flooding my mind. But they just kept coming.

"This cross is too heavy," I whispered as tears began cascading down my face and onto the carpet beneath me. "Please, Jesus, please—it's too heavy."

I spent the rest of the night on the floor, vacillating between disbelief, despair, and rage, before finally falling into a fitful sleep on the couch. John left early for work—he had to pull a thirty-six-hour shift at the hospital, so I would not see him until the next evening—and I found myself facing another interminable day and night by myself. Writing alone in my home office was out of the question, so I stepped out into our suburban, kid-saturated neighborhood for a walk. Every swing set and stray tricycle I spotted reduced me to tears again. I tried to call a friend on my cell phone but wound up sobbing on the sidewalk before I could tell her what was wrong. I was a wreck. And all I saw stretching before me was more of the same—more misery, tears, and waiting for a child that might never come.

I never knew how much I wanted to be a mother until I realized I might not have the chance. Overnight, the imaginary child I had begrudged for cramping my style became the Holy Grail. The maternal desires I had ignored for years while defending my independence and pursuing my career suddenly came roaring back, threatening to devour me with their primal intensity.

The ensuing months brought more tears, terror, and tests. Shortly after we received that initial scare, follow-up tests conducted by the same physician generated normal results. The next month, another round of tests produced more signs of potential problems, and the roller-coaster ride resumed. I soon learned that fertility medicine is more art than science, and an aggravating art at that. Everything is about probabilities and percentages, trial and error. John and I might be able to conceive a child together, or we might not. The only way to know for sure was if I found a plus sign on one of those little pregnancy-test sticks that now cluttered the back of my bathroom closet.

Month after agonizing month, I locked myself in the bathroom, made the sign of the cross, and stared at that stick for three minutes, awaiting a miracle. Month after month, the stick stared back at me with nothing more to show for all my prayers, pleas, and doctor visits than a defiant minus sign. John would find me sobbing on the bathroom floor, wondering why, just once, that damned stick could not give me a plus sign.

Those negative test results and the telltale menstrual cramps that confirmed them always seemed to arrive at the worst times. They would come just as I was heading to a baby shower, chatting with a friend who called to tell me she was expecting, or lying alone in a hotel room in a strange city where I had traveled for just the sort of prestigious speaking engagement that I had once coveted more than a child. My cramps frequently kicked in as I was taking the podium to deliver a pro-life speech or stepping under the camera lights to conduct an interview on Catholic bioethics for *Faith & Culture,* my new talk show on the Eternal Word Television Network. No matter when they hit, they left me racked with pain inside and out, brokenhearted at God's refusal to grant me success in this one part of life that now mattered more to me than any other.

From my status as a loser in the fertility lottery, it was not much of a leap to conclude that I was a failure as a woman as well. If the ability to conceive and bear children is the defining biological fact of the female body, what did it say about me that my body had failed to fulfill this function? What did it say about my marriage to John that our union had proven fruitless? Did it mean that God had not meant for us to marry? That my return to St. Louis had been a mistake? That the supernatural nudges I had felt in recent years—to focus more on family and less on work—had been illusions? And what of the Catholic teachings on reproduction that I had defended so publicly: Was my predicament proof that they were not as wise or universal as I had thought? It was one thing to embrace those teachings as a beaming newlywed whose biggest worry is having too many bundles of joy. It was quite another to do so when facing the possibility that following them—especially the church's ban on in vitro fertilization—might mean never conceiving a child.

John and I kept our fertility struggles hidden from all but a handful of loved ones. We figured we did not need the added burden of being publicly labeled barren or pumped for updates from curious friends and relatives. Although sharing this painful secret drew us closer, I could not help noticing how differently we reacted to our ongoing struggle. John could shake off the monthly disappointments more quickly than I could, losing himself in his work and keeping our infertility troubles quarantined from the rest of life. For me, the problem pervaded my consciousness. As I monitored my body's daily fertility signs, felt my spirits rise and fall with each hormone fluctuation, planned my days around my debilitating cramps and frequent doctors' visits, offered my arms as pincushions to an ever-changing cast of phlebotomists, and served as ground zero for nearly every treatment that we pursued, regardless of what problem the doctors suspected was causing our troubles, I felt keenly the burden that comes from being not just a childless person but a childless woman.

That burden extended beyond the bounds of the doctor's office. Nosy strangers who knew nothing of John's or my medical history routinely attributed our failure to reproduce to me and peppered me with questions they would never ask John. I faced the most humiliating pop quizzes in the socially conservative religious circles where I often worked and socialized. I was shocked at how many otherwise thoughtful, polite Christians thought nothing of scolding me publicly for my childlessness, convinced that my career was the reason John and I had failed to be fruitful and multiply. Married two years and still no kids? Hadn't I heard about the glories of the pro-child NFP lifestyle and the dangers of popping the pill? Didn't I know I wasn't getting any younger? That all this career business, nice as it was, wasn't the real point of a woman's life or her marriage?

The only thing worse than grillings from anti-contraception crusaders who pegged me for a cafeteria Catholic were those from armchair experts who had guessed our predicament and wanted to help me solve it—usually in the middle of a crowded cocktail party, at the front of the line at one of my book signings, or in the pew as I tried to pray alone after Mass. Their questions were similarly obvious and unhelpful: Had I seen a doctor? Those NFP-only physicians can work fertility miracles, you know. Maybe I should just relax; God will send me a child if it's his will. Could it be he doesn't want me to be a mother? Besides, there's always adoption. Had I heard about that woman who tried to get pregnant for years? As soon as she and her husband filled out the adoption papers, poof! She conceived!

I usually felt too frozen with embarrassment to respond to such comments. I would simply smile and nod, silently begging God to make this person shut up and go away. I knew the advice stemmed from a desire to help. Yet most comments I heard, even from friends and family, only disheartened me more. They minimized my longing for a baby, making me feel silly and ashamed for taking my childlessness so hard. And they never addressed my deepest question about infertility: Why had God given me these maternal desires if he never intended to fulfill them?

## Kindred Spirits

In the spring of 2006, while John and I were immersed in our ongoing quest for a child, I got a call from a friend. She was planning a women's luncheon to raise funds for a local after-school program her daughter attended. Would I be willing to serve as keynote speaker and address some topic of significance to Christian women today?

I was interested but a little hesitant to accept. I had attended the previous year's luncheon before my infertility crisis began, and even then I felt out of place in the crowd of well-heeled, mostly stay-at-home mothers. The keynote speech had focused on faith and fashion—not a gripping topic for someone who still wears shirts she bought in high school and typically jumps on trend bandwagons just as everyone else is jumping off. I cringed when the speaker began by congratulating her audience on choosing the season's hottest new pastel-colored flouncy skirts and pumps over dark hues and pants, a sure sign that they cherished their femininity. There I was at the head table, sporting a five-year-old black pantsuit with dowdy flats and feeling like Bella Abzug trapped at a Tupperware party. Things went downhill from there.

I knew the women who attended this annual luncheon were sincere in their faith and desire to glorify God through their femininity. But I had no interest in telling them how to look pretty for Jesus or channel their inner June Cleaver. So I told my friend that I would speak to them if I could tackle a topic that interested me: a Catholic view of womanhood as articulated by John Paul and a saint he recently had canonized, Edith Stein.

My motives were mostly selfish. I had spent months trying to find resources to help me make sense of my womanhood in light of my faith and fertility struggles. Most of what I had read in Christian books and magazines struck me as too pious and peppy, a baptized version of the same here's-some-baby-dust, you'll-conceive-any-day-now messages that turned me off secular infertility chat rooms. I thought that digging into the meatier reflections of these two Catholic luminaries might prove more helpful. The speech gave me an excuse—and a deadline—to do so.

I began my research by revisiting John Paul's writings on women: his 1988 apostolic letter, *On the Dignity and Vocation of Women,* his 1995 *Letter to Women,* and his 1995 encyclical, *The Gospel of Life,* in which he first called for a new, pro-life, Christian feminism to "affirm the true genius of women in every aspect of the life of society." Although the pope's thoughts on women were not new to me, poring over them again reminded me how unequivocal he was about the equal dignity of the sexes and the need for women to share their gifts with the church and society, not just the family.

This time around, I paid particular attention to John Paul's emphasis on the concept of spiritual maternity, the idea that women harbor a natural inclination to welcome the human person and to "see persons with their hearts . . . independently of various ideological or political systems . . . in their greatness and limitations." The pope describes this person-centered, maternal character of a woman's heart as the essence of true femininity. This struck me as a refreshingly substantive definition of femininity, far more appealing than the frilly-and-sassy stereotype so common at women's conferences and in the women's spirituality aisle of most bookstores. Even more appealing was John Paul's claim that a woman can discover and cultivate spiritual maternity regardless of her state in life or her ability to bear children, though pregnancy can heighten her awareness of this gift. Every woman is called to be a mother, the pope says, but there is more than one way to answer that call.

This new understanding of motherhood fascinated me. I yearned to learn more, to see the idea of spiritual maternity fleshed out more fully. So I turned to a book on my shelf that I had been meaning to dive into, a collection of writings on women by Jewish-born philosopher, Catholic convert, and Carmelite nun Edith Stein. I already had read Edith's unfinished autobiography, *Life in a Jewish Family*, which chronicles her early years in Germany. That book offers little insight into Edith's faith-based philosophy of women because its narrative ends abruptly before her adult conversion to Christianity. Edith meant to write more, but she was forced to quit writing on August 2, 1942. That's when the Gestapo raided her convent as part of a roundup in Holland of all Catholics of Jewish descent, who were targeted in retaliation for an anti-Nazi pastoral letter published a week earlier by the Dutch bishops. The Nazis arrested Edith and put her on a cattle car to Auschwitz. A week later she was dead.

I visited Auschwitz in 2002, while touring Poland. Walking along the train tracks that led more than a million prisoners into the deadly camp and standing in the gas chamber where most of them died, I gained a new appreciation for the horrors of the Holocaust and the suffering of its individual victims, including Edith. I later learned that controversy had surrounded John Paul's decision to canonize Edith a martyr in 1998, because some Jews considered it an attempt to "Christianize" the Holocaust by attributing Edith's death to her Catholic identity as well as her Jewish roots. For her part, Edith saw her conversion to Catholicism as a fulfillment, not repudiation, of her Jewish heritage. An eminent philosopher before entering the convent, she spoke out publicly against the Nazis and implored Pope Pius XII to do the same. Fellow prisoners described her as courageous and consoling as she traveled to her death, forgetful of herself and tenderly feeding and bathing infants whose mothers had lost hope. Edith grieved more for her Jewish people than for herself, one survivor said, and looked like "a Pietà without the Christ."

Compelling as I found the circumstances of Edith's death, what I learned in researching her life and other writings intrigued me even more. For starters, we shared similar conversion stories. Not that similar, of course: Edith was born into a Jewish family nearly a century before me and lapsed into atheism before ultimately reading her way into the Catholic Church. But the story that marked a turning point in her adult faith journey was the same one that had jump-started mine: the life of Saint Teresa of Ávila, which Edith devoured in one night before closing the book and declaring, "This is the truth."

Truth mattered to Edith. She spent her life searching for it, first in the study of psychology, then in the budding philosophical movement known as phenomenology, which emphasizes careful reflection on personal experience in the pursuit of truth. Inspired by Teresa and the witness of some Christian friends, Edith's search ultimately led her to the church, where scripture and the philosophy of Saint Thomas Aquinas gave her a fuller picture of the dignity and destiny of the human person.

Among the questions that intrigued Edith throughout her scholarly career in philosophy were those related to the nature of woman. A self-proclaimed feminist with little patience for superficial or chauvinist views of femininity, Edith lauded the advances that women had made in her day. Yet she saw dangers in feminist efforts to downplay what she called "feminine singularity," the unique inclinations that women possess by virtue of being women. Although Edith believed that men and women share the same basic human traits and eternal destiny, she saw significant differences in the way they relate to God, the world, and their own bodies. She considered it crucial that a woman understand her distinctively feminine nature in order to live in harmony with it.

Edith's insightful reflections on women's issues made her a beloved teacher to young women and the intellectual leader of the European Catholic women's movement in the 1930s. Those reflections, published in English as *Essays on Woman,* capture the essence of woman as only the work of another woman can. They deal with themes ranging from the sublime—such as the role of woman in salvation history—to the mundane—such as how a woman can avoid losing touch with her feminine gifts while working in a male-dominated field. And at their heart lies a view of motherhood that poses a profound challenge to women in all walks of life.

## Blessed Motherhood

Like John Paul, a fellow philosopher who went on to echo some of her themes in his *Theology of the Body,* Edith grounds many of her insights on the biblical creation accounts and the body. In Genesis, she pays particular attention to woman's designation as a "suitable partner" for man and God's command that man and woman "be fertile and multiply" and become "one flesh" (Gen. 2:18, 1:28, and 2:24). She reads those verses as confirmation that woman has a natural calling to be a spouse and mother. This inborn orientation to be a companion to another and to nurture another's physical, emotional, intellectual, or spiritual growth can be fulfilled most obviously through marriage and motherhood, Edith says, but also through the consecrated life and self-giving work in the world.

Edith finds support for this calling in the structure of a woman's body, which is designed to be receptive to both a man and a child. Edith believes this physical receptivity reveals a spiritual openness to the human person imprinted on a woman's soul. "The deepest longing of woman's heart is to give herself lovingly, to belong to another, and to possess this other being completely," Edith writes. "This longing is revealed in her outlook, personal and all-embracing, which appears to us as specifically feminine."

Although men are also called to loving communion with others, Edith considers man's nature more oriented than woman's to "action, work, and objective achievements." A man, she says, "is less concerned with problems of being, whether his own or of others." He has a more intense drive for individual, objective achievements, Edith says, because of his heightened capacity to submit himself to an external discipline and focus exclusively on the attainment of a specific goal. She believes that this capacity helps a man in his role as a father because it inclines him to push his child to "make good" and gives him the drive to protect and provide for his family.

A woman's body and soul, by contrast, "are fashioned less to fight and to conquer than to cherish, guard and preserve." Edith believed that women possess a more holistic outlook on life than men, partly because they are bound more closely to their bodies through their menstrual cycles, pregnancy, and the physical demands of motherhood, which make them less likely to lose themselves in abstraction. Edith says that women tend to pay more attention to persons than to things, to relationships and the concrete reality of people's lives than to theories, and to the whole truth of a person or situation than to an analysis of its parts. While a man often gets preoccupied with his own "enterprise," Edith says, a woman's innate desire to be a companion and mother makes her delight in sharing the details and daily concerns of her loved ones—concerns that matter to her simply because they matter to someone she loves.

A woman's tendency toward openness to others also inclines her toward intense and loving union with God. Edith sees women as natural contemplatives in the world because they have a knack for blending attentiveness to concrete tasks with a capacity for cultivating silence and peace. She notes that women frequently yearn for an integrated life in which their spiritual, intellectual, emotional, and practical concerns merge and they can connect their faith to everyday tasks. Prayerful surrender to God amid daily life suits a woman's soul, Edith says, and this surrender "represents the highest fulfillment of all feminine aspirations . . . Correctly speaking, it is the highest fulfillment of our human vocation; but this is felt more vividly and sought more directly by the woman because it is in accordance with her specific nature."

Some of Edith's claims about women's specific characteristics, including her remarks about a woman's "subordinate" and "emotional" nature, seem dated and smack of the rigidly defined archetypes of Carl Jung, a theorist who achieved prominence during the time Edith studied psychology. Yet Edith acknowledges that the tendencies she describes vary according to individuals, with some men manifesting inclinations ascribed to women more than some women do and vice versa. She does not believe that a woman's person-focused outlook limits her to working in the so-called "helping professions" or that all women must marry and bear children. Edith herself pursued a challenging scholarly career in a field dominated by men and lived for decades as a single woman in the world, before entering the convent and embracing a martyr's death. She insists that a woman's maternal orientation calls her to be not only nurturing and generous but also knowledgeable, strong, and brave, to stand and fight as only a mother can when she sees her children attacked.

A biblical example of this loving, generous, and brave maternal ideal can be found in Mary, the mother of Jesus. Edith sees Mary as a model mother not only because she conceived Jesus in her womb but because she first conceived him in her heart. In answering God's audacious request with her simple fiat—"Let it be done unto me according to your word" (Luke 1:38)—Mary modeled the radical openness to the human person that God wants from every woman and every disciple. Jesus suggests as much in his answer to the woman in the crowd in Luke's Gospel, when she calls out to him, "Blessed is the womb that bore you, and the breasts that you sucked." He corrects her: "Blessed, rather, are those who hear the word of God and keep it" (Luke 11:27–28). Jesus says this not to denigrate Mary's physical motherhood but to emphasize that what God values above all is receptivity to his will—the very receptivity, Edith notes, that is exemplified in Mary.

## Daughters of Eve

Mary is a tough act to follow, as Edith acknowledges. Unlike the mother of Jesus, the rest of us are tainted by sinful tendencies that can turn our greatest strengths into our greatest weaknesses. Edith sees a foreshadowing of sin's distorting effect in the sex-specific curses that God metes out to Adam and Eve after the fall:

> To the woman he said: "I will intensify the pangs of your childbearing; in pain shall you bring forth children. Yet your urge shall be for your husband, and he shall be your master." To the man he said: "Because you listened to your wife and ate from the tree of which I had forbidden you to eat, cursed be the ground because of you! In toil shall you eat its yield all the days of your life. Thorns and thistles shall it bring forth to you, as you eat of the plants of the field. By the sweat of your face shall you get bread to eat, until you return to the ground, from which you were taken; for you are dirt, and to dirt you shall return."
>
> *Gen. 3:16–19*

For men, Edith believes, this passage hints at two sins to which they are especially prone: the domination of women and obsession with work. Edith argues that sin turns a man's drive for achievement into a disordered desire for perfection that can degrade both man and his surroundings. He may adopt a materialistic worldview that pays no heed to goods that cannot be counted or seen. He may reject any limits on his freedom and inquiry and refuse to submit to laws outside himself. This cycle of grasping and destroying can even extend into the natural environment, Edith says, when "instead of reverential joy in the created world, instead of a desire to preserve and develop it, man seeks to exploit it greedily to the point of destruction or to senseless acquisition without understanding how to profit from it or how to enjoy it."

For women, Edith considers telling the reference to a woman's "urge" for the husband who would be her "master." It suggests that while men are more tempted to make work or money their god, women are prone to making idols of other people and relationships. A woman's natural focus on persons can metastasize into nosiness and gossip, Edith says, "a perverse desire to penetrate into personal lives, a passion of wanting to confiscate people." Her attentiveness to loved ones can lead to smothering and a "false pursuit of prestige" that drives her to stake her self-worth on the success of her husband or children. Her desire to serve others can tempt her to take on too much and fail to meet her primary responsibilities or distinguish her own identity from those she serves.

Sin can warp the gifts that dispose a woman toward intimacy with God and others. Her heightened sensitivity can devolve into touchiness and sentimentality. The natural unity between body and soul that orients her toward a holistic faith and awareness of what's happening inside her can lapse into a fixation on creature comforts and mindless pleasure seeking. Even her knack for balancing diverse interests and duties can degenerate, Edith says, into "a perverted desire for totality and inclusiveness, a mania to know everything and thereby to skim the surface of everything and to plunge deeply into nothing."

This is woman's maternal gift gone awry, her natural assets twisted into liabilities. When this happens, the generous, selfless mother becomes the controlling matriarch with a martyr complex whom no one can please. The attentive, inquisitive friend becomes the insatiable busybody who smears reputations for sport. The affectionate wife becomes the resentful nag who cannot forgive her husband for failing to meet her every emotional need. And the young woman who longs for a child to love becomes the covetous fertility consumer bitter at God and the world for failing to supply her with the baby she knows she deserves. In each case, a woman's longing for God's infinite love has been misdirected to human beings, with disastrous results.

Edith suggests two remedies for a woman who finds herself falling into this trap. The first is what she calls "thoroughly objective work," which consists of anything from sweeping the kitchen floor to balancing a budget or researching a term paper. Such work forces a woman to submit to laws outside herself, helps her escape her obsessive focus on herself and her own emotions, and encourages her to develop self-control, an important discipline for the spiritual life.

The second remedy is even more crucial: structuring one's days in a way that opens doors to God's grace. Fidelity to Christ and to the demands of one's vocation requires "intense spiritual stamina," Edith notes, and that stamina "perishes in the long run if not refreshed by the eternal wellspring" of grace. She believes that a woman should tap into that wellspring through frequent sacramental confession, regular reception of Holy Communion, and quiet prayer throughout the day, preferably in the presence of the Eucharist.

Edith recommends that a woman should, if possible, attend Mass in the morning and ask Jesus after receiving him in the Eucharist how he wants her to spend her day. As the day progresses and new worries and problems accumulate, she should take a noontime break to reconnect with God. A Eucharistic holy hour or solitary rest in a quiet place is ideal, Edith says, but if that's impossible, she should take a moment to "seal herself off inwardly against all other things and take refuge in the Lord. He is indeed there and can give us in a single moment what we need." The day's work and problems will continue, but we will remain at peace. Edith writes: "And when night comes, and retrospect shows that everything was patchwork and much which one had planned left undone, when so many things rouse shame and regret, then take all as it is, lay it in God's hands, and offer it up to him. In this way we will be able to rest in him, actually to rest, and to begin the new day like a new life."

A woman who follows these natural rhythms of prayer, work, and rest will be rewarded with abiding peace, Edith says. She will find in Jesus a worthy outlet for her feminine longing to lose herself in love: "The surrender to which feminine nature inclines is here appropriate; on the other hand, we also *find* here the absolute love and surrender for which we seek vainly in people. And surrender to Christ does not make us blind and deaf to the needs of others—on the contrary. We now seek for God's image in each human being and want, above all, to help each human being win his freedom."

Genuine spiritual motherhood lies in leading others to freedom, not dependence; in giving, not getting. But a woman cannot give what she does not first possess. Only in loving union with God can she find the strength and selflessness she needs to be a true spiritual mother. A woman's craving for God's love is a not a weakness, Edith says. It is her greatest strength: "The *intrinsic value of woman* consists essentially in *exceptional receptivity for God's work in the soul.*"

## Seeing Spiritual Maternity

Edith's insights resonated deeply with me, opening my eyes to truths I had intuited for years but never put into words. I found them especially helpful in making sense of my maternal desires and sorrow over infertility. Finally, I had found someone who took seriously my desperation to conceive a child in my womb, who saw my yearning for biological motherhood as a reasonable response to the way God had fashioned me, physically and spiritually. Edith's observations about the close connection between a woman's body and her soul helped me understand why I found it more difficult than John to ignore or compartmentalize our fertility troubles. My monthly periods, and the subtle changes I noticed in my body all month long, kept me continually conscious of the fact that I was not pregnant.

Even as Edith's views validated my suffering, they challenged me to rethink my fixation on getting pregnant. If motherhood is more about what's in your heart than what's in your womb, I needed to stop waiting for a baby to use my maternal gifts. I needed to start recognizing the opportunities I already had to nurture growth in others, defend the vulnerable, and make the world a more loving, humane place.

The prospect frightened me. Since John and I received our first dose of bad news on the fertility front, I had careened between mourning my maternal desires and fighting to suppress them. My frustration at our failure to conceive had often led me to neglect prayer and escape into the excesses Edith warned against: superficiality, covetousness, and the pursuit of prestige.

My escapes took subtle forms. I would spend a few weeks quietly fixating on my weight and clothes, bitterly deciding that if my body could not produce a baby, it must be thinner, sexier, and more stunning than all those bodies that could. I would immerse myself in lavish travel plans, concluding that if John and I were going to be perceived as materialistic yuppies with no interest in children, we might as well play the part. I would dive into my work, not with the sense of duty and balance Edith extolled but with the explicit intention of working too many hours, garnering too many accolades, and earning too much applause to feel the pain of missing out on motherhood—or to feel much of anything, for that matter. None of my escapes lasted for long. I always wound up back at square one, weeping in the bathroom over that accursed pregnancy stick.

The strategies Edith suggested for coping with trials made more sense. I knew from experience that turning my mind to work helped when I found myself mired in self-pity, provided I maintained the balance between prayer, work, and rest that Edith advocated. The sacraments had been a source of strength to me for years, but Edith's concrete suggestions about prayer reminded me to check in with Jesus throughout the day just as I checked in with John. Her warning against false idols particularly hit home, as I realized that the child I wanted so badly had become one for me.

I began to watch for openings to exercise spiritual maternity in my own life. I did not have to look far. The more active role I had taken in my father's care since I had returned to St. Louis from DC allowed me to practice plenty of patience and nurturing. I finally understood the source of that satisfaction that filled me those times that I held Dad's hand as he walked unsteadily, combed his thinning hair when he had forgotten, and encouraged him as he read to me, for the umpteenth time, an excerpt of scripture from the breviary page he had forgotten to turn. For so long, I had assumed that caring for Dad had nothing to do with longing for motherhood, even though my sorrow over infertility curiously abated whenever I visited my father. Now I realized that while I had been giving Dad my attention, he had been giving me an experience of motherhood.

Discovering Edith inspired me to approach the substance of my work differently, too. Her description of a woman's "personal and all-embracing" outlook shed new light on my desire to make my writing more personal, to integrate my work and faith more fully, and to nurture growth in my readers, rather than simply winning debates. I had tried to squelch this desire in the past, fearing that a more personal, creative turn in my work would make me more vulnerable to criticism. Reading Edith emboldened me to reconsider. Perhaps the drive to bear fruit that I could not satisfy on a physical level could spill over into my work and make it more poignant, resonant, and real. Maybe I could give myself permission to be more open about who I was and what I believed, to be truly maternal in my willingness to give to others until it hurt.

Searching for signs of spiritual maternity in myself led me to start seeing this gift in other women, as well. I saw it in my friend

Judy, a single theology teacher at a Philadelphia Catholic high school who gave unreservedly of her time, counsel, and prayers to the current and former students whom she cherished like daughters. I saw it in my friend Marisa, whose passion for spreading the Gospel and defending the vulnerable had led her to join the Sisters of Life, a budding, New York–based religious order whose sisters lived simply while caring with maternal solicitude for pregnant women and their children who had nowhere else to turn. I even saw it in strangers, like the pair of women I spotted once outside the Shrine of the Most Blessed Sacrament in Hanceville, Alabama, where a life-sized, bloodied corpus of Christ hung from a cross. Many pilgrims had passed right by that crucifix, but when these women encountered it, their hands flew to their mouths and they stood, silently weeping, for nearly a half hour. As I watched them gently caress those porcelain wounds and whisper to Jesus how they wished they could take away his pain, I finally understood the exquisite beauty of the weeping women who kept Christ company on Calvary.

Closer to home, I saw spiritual maternity in my own mother, who bore the lion's share of the burden of caring for my father. Since his Alzheimer's diagnosis a decade earlier, he had become more of a child to her than a husband. Mom would bathe Dad and dress him, toilet him and clean up his messes, feed him and pray with him—all while holding down a full-time job to support him financially. She leaned on Jesus to make it through her exhausting days and kept this message posted on her mirror to put her burden in perspective: "Today, a little work. Tomorrow, eternal rest."

Mom's burden was bearing fruit, more than she knew. Friends and strangers frequently told me how much they had learned about love by observing Mom's solicitous, meticulous care for Dad. I had learned, too. Watching her gently coax my father to eat his vegetables, giggle with him at whatever caught his fancy, or tuck him in at night while reciting his favorite Guardian Angel prayer from childhood, I realized that there is nothing second-rate about spiritual motherhood. It is a powerful channel of God's love in a love-starved world, one all the more potent when it springs from trials you do not choose.

## "Make Me a Baby"

None of these insights erased the pain of my childlessness. Two years after John and I began trying to conceive, I ached as ever for a baby and felt frustrated that we still seemed no closer to conceiving or understanding why we could not conceive than when we began. Our search for better answers began to lead us beyond the Catholic, NFP-only physicians we initially had consulted into the wild-and-wooly world of secular fertility specialists who did IVF as a matter of course. We had no intention of flouting church teaching, as we made clear to each new doctor we saw, but neither did we believe that our Catholic faith confined us to consulting only physicians with papal portraits hanging in their offices and papal encyclicals tucked between their medical textbooks.

The gulf between the two types of physicians was jarring, though. The fertility clinics we visited were the opposite of the NFP offices we had seen: large, hyperefficient, and loaded with patients willing to spend whatever they had and do whatever it took to conceive. I felt like a medieval throwback sitting in those plush lobbies, refusing even to discuss IVF with doctors who proposed it as the default answer to nearly every fertility problem and trying not to stare when I saw women old enough to be my mother passing through the doors, wearing the same desperate look and seeking the same shot at pregnancy as I did. I did not know their stories; perhaps they had been riding this miserable merry-go-round much longer than I had. But I could not help feeling irked that their conception odds might beat mine, since they could consider treatments that I, as an obedient Catholic, could not.

Once, while sitting in the hallway of such a clinic, I saw an Asian woman in her late thirties come face-to-face with a doctor. He complimented her on the infant in her stroller—a blue-eyed, blond-haired baby who bore no resemblance to her, possibly due to the use of donor eggs—and she thanked him. Then she told him that she had returned to see him because, she said, "it's time for you to make me another baby."

Her words made me flinch. I thought: Isn't God the author of life? Isn't it wrong to think of a baby as a product to be manufactured to your specifications and on your timetable, rather than a gift to be received from the hands of the Creator? I could imagine the woman's response, because somewhere in the back of my mind I had said it myself: I gave God a chance. Now it's time for the doctors and me to make this happen, whether God likes it or not.

I knew such a covetous view of children clashed with my deepest values and my growing awareness of what it truly meant to be a mother. Still, I resented the limits that Catholic teaching imposed on John and me. I knew that scores of Catholics ignore those limits, and I even had heard from a priest in the confessional that I should do the same. I knew better than to put much stock in his patently unorthodox advice, even if it did come in the middle of a pilgrimage that John and I had taken to ask God for a child.

Sometimes, though, I just felt like a chump. Here I was, trying to honor both my Catholic convictions and my maternal desires. And I was catching flack from all sides: traditional Catholics who looked askance at both childlessness and nearly any fertility treatment beyond reciting the rosary, secular doctors who regarded my religious beliefs with bewilderment bordering on contempt, and assorted friends and relatives who, never having experienced infertility, could not figure out why John and I didn't just drop all this medical mumbo jumbo and adopt—as if adoption were a panacea for the pain of infertility, a choice that should be easy and automatic for every infertile couple. I recognized adoption as a loving and generous calling that had built beautiful families, and I realized that God might call John and me to adopt someday. But I saw adoption as just that: a calling, one that not every couple receives and that demands its own discernment process. Why did people who had rejoiced in their own biological children and never considered adoption themselves feel entitled to judge infertile couples like us for feeling the same natural desire to reproduce they had felt—and for focusing our energy on fulfilling that desire even in the face of serious obstacles?

When resentment threatened to overwhelm me, I tried to focus on the wisdom of Catholic bioethics and the seamless way that the church's teachings on love, sex, marriage, and parenthood fit together. The church's insistence that spouses remain open to new life in every sexual act reminds them that their love is about more than their own gratification; it is meant to mirror in the world the generosity and fruitfulness of God himself. I knew that the church's refusal to sanction fertility treatments that sever the link between sex and baby-making testified to a similar truth: that children are not commodities to be produced but gifts to be received. Catholic teaching says married couples can use only those fertility treatments that assist, rather than replace, the role of a couple's sexual union in creating new life in the womb. Correctly applying that principle can take some sleuthing; John and I found the National Catholic Bioethics Center to be a reliable resource for up-to-date, medically informed, orthodox Catholic answers about what the church does and does not allow. But IVF clearly crosses the line, since it involves the conception of an embryo *in vitro*—literally, in glass—rather than in the mother's womb.

I knew well the social consequences that followed from ignoring the church's limits on fertility treatments. I studied, wrote, and spoke about them all the time. Reproductive technologies that had begun as a means of alleviating the suffering of infertile adults had led to the increasing objectification of their unborn children. There were the so-called leftover embryos from IVF clinics that scientists now used as disposable research material. There were the children produced through donor eggs, donor sperm, and surrogate wombs, often born into intentionally fatherless or motherless families and deprived of the chance to know both biological parents. Unlike orphans and adoptees, these "donor babies" had to live with the knowledge that the very parents raising them were the ones who intentionally brought them into the world in a way that virtually guaranteed they would never know their biological mothers or fathers. And then there were the bizarre stories about the Brave New World of assisted reproduction that surfaced almost daily: tales of sexagenarians bearing triplets; women acting as surrogate birth mothers to their own grandchildren; parents using prenatal testing to weed out defective embryos and fetuses they did not want—including girls when they wanted a boy and vice versa; parents demanding "designer babies" and breeding "savior siblings" for the express purpose of mining their bodies for tissues or organs that older siblings needed.

IVF's role in opening the door to all of these excesses bothered me. Its role in enabling embryo-destructive research troubled me most. The IVF-inspired view of human embryos as commodities, and the growing demand for more disposable embryos than IVF clinics could furnish, had fueled a push for cloning experiments among researchers who now wanted to manufacture an endless supply of unborn human beings explicitly for this purpose. Proponents of these clone-and-kill experiments dismissed the objections of a squeamish public by arguing that the embryos involved were not truly human clones, because they would be destroyed long before they could be implanted in wombs and grow into "real" babies.

I knew all about this research because moneyed interests in my own state recently had passed a ballot initiative to make it a constitutional right. Appalled by their misleading campaign ads, I had served as an outspoken opponent of the initiative in local and national media. I knew I could not separate my opposition to the creation of human embryos in a lab dish for research from my opposition to the creation of human embryos in a test tube for reproduction. If one contradicted the human person's intrinsic dignity, then so did the other. I would be a hypocrite if I publicly condemned one while privately doing the other.

All my knowledge only took me so far, however. Like the vision of motherhood that I had found in Edith's writings, the wisdom of Catholic bioethics that warmed my heart still left me with the problem of my empty womb.

One winter day in early 2007, that problem led John and me to consult a new physician, a highly recommended fertility specialist at a local Catholic hospital. John had explained to his receptionist when making the appointment that we had no interest in IVF, and she assured him that would not be an issue.

It was. After glancing briefly through our file filled with conflicting test results and competing theories about our essentially unexplained infertility, the doctor launched into a hard sell about what perfect candidates we were for IVF. When I reminded him that we already had ruled out IVF for religious reasons, he lit into me, firing off questions about my ethical objections and ridiculing me for my archaic beliefs. By the time we ended the meeting, the doctor was hollering, predicting that we would never—mark his words, *never*—conceive without IVF.

John and I walked briskly to the parking lot. Stunned and smarting at the physician's rudeness, I tried to make sense of what I had heard. Was it really true? Had I really reached the point where IVF was my only option to conceive? That night, I popped into John's office and we began to chat about what had happened. At first, we ranted about the doctor and his hubris. Soon, though, we were railing about our entire ordeal: the injustice of our infertility, the insensitivity of those who chided us for our childlessness, the attempts we had made to use fertility treatments allowed by the church, only to see them fail. Was IVF really that much different, after all we had been through? Was our commitment to following an unpopular, largely ignored church teaching worth sacrificing our only chance at having a biological child?

We had vented these frustrations before. When I groused, John would remind me that there was still hope, that God would bless our decision to obey him. When John grumbled, I would tell him the same. This time, neither of us played God's advocate. We complained our way into a corner, then fell into a troubled silence, leaving unsaid what we were, for the first time, actually contemplating.

The next morning I rose early for a walk through our neighborhood, the one we had chosen specifically for its family friendliness. As I passed each swing set and stroller, I thought of the ways my life would change if we tried IVF. After years of waiting, I might finally have a child—a child formed of my very flesh and that of the man I loved. I could end my exhausting treks to fertility clinics, the anguished rounds of conception roulette that left me in tears every month, the humiliation of constantly apologizing for my childlessness everywhere I went. I could stand up in church for the Mother's Day blessing instead of cowering in my pew, teary and ashamed. I could send out baby announcements and family-photo Christmas cards instead of feeling a lump form in my throat every time someone else's arrived at my door. I could feel the thrill of seeing a plus sign on that pregnancy-test stick, sensing a tiny foot kicking in my womb, swaddling a sweet, whimpering newborn in my arms, suckling a baby at my breast. I could experience with John the joys of recognizing ourselves in a child who shared our features and family traits, growing old surrounded by the family we had created together, and knowing that taste of immortality that comes from living on through your children and grandchildren. I could be a mother at last. And no one would have to know how it happened.

As I strolled past the day-care center I passed every morning, the one that always made me wonder what use my work-from-home career was since I had no children to stay home for, I shivered. The breeze that rustled my hair felt colder than it had when

I left the house. I noticed a faded yard sign amid a pile of leaves across the street, one that pledged a "no" vote on the cloning amendment that had passed the previous fall. I started to think of all the other changes that would come if John and I used IVF.

I had felt inklings of them already in the uneasy silence that had descended on us since our conversation ended the night before. Although pregnancy might be within reach with IVF, it would come at the cost of the deep, underlying peace that had pervaded my life and my marriage amid the most tempestuous trials—the peace of living in harmony with John, my own conscience, and what I thought God wanted of me.

I knew God could forgive me for choosing IVF. I knew that if he allowed me to conceive a child using IVF, he would love that child as much as one conceived according to his plan. Yet I also knew my relationship with him would never be the same if I purposely made such a fundamental, life-altering choice against what I knew to be his will for me. I suspected that the presence of a child conceived through IVF always would be tinged with sadness for me, since it would remind me that, at a critical juncture in my life, I had chosen my need for control over God's invitation to trust.

I thought back to that woman in the clinic who wanted the doctor to make her another baby. How could she view her child as a person who existed for his own sake and not for hers, when she had ordered his creation to suit her needs and her time line? Perhaps she could hold those two ideas in tension: child as carefully crafted, promptly delivered product and child as unmerited blessing. As for me, I knew I could not. I had to choose between them. If I staked my dreams of motherhood on my belief that an unborn child must never be treated as a mere choice to be created or destroyed at will, I would risk childlessness. But I could put that risk in God's hands, confident that whatever children he eventually gave me—biological, adoptive, or spiritual—I would embrace them with a clear conscience and an open heart, knowing that they belonged to him, not me.

I felt a burst of energy as I turned the corner and began my trek back home. When I arrived, I found John sitting at his desk, his face looking lighter and more peaceful than I had seen it in weeks. He had been praying through the scripture verses in his breviary that morning and had reached the same conclusion. Either we would conceive a child in a way we could live with, or we would not conceive at all. We would continue to seek medical help but IVF would remain off the table, no matter what the doctors said.

"God will take care of us," John whispered as we hugged, and I knew it was true.

## In God's Eyes

The weather was still chilly on the May morning when I found myself pacing in a northern-Wisconsin parking lot, trying to find a sweet spot in the gray sky overhead where my cell phone would work. My mother and I were traveling together, taking a break from visiting my grandmother in her Green Bay nursing home. A meandering drive southward had brought us to the Spanish-style Carmelite Monastery of the Holy Name of Jesus, which was perched amid gentle hills near Lake Michigan's shore. I was eager to peek inside at the chapel, but first I wanted to check the messages I had received while roaming out of range.

I finally found a pocket of reception and heard the frantic voice of a Fox News producer who recently had added me to her Rolodex of go-to pundits for live TV interviews. She was planning a debate segment on a breaking news topic that day, something right up my alley. She could find a TV station for me to use wherever I was if I could carve out an hour or so for a live shot. She needed to hear from me right away. Was I in?

I paused for an instant, wondering how I might squeeze this into my weekend, then quickly thought better of it and called her up to politely decline. "I'll be unavailable all weekend," I told her when she asked if the next day was an option. "I'm tied up with family."

After hanging up, I took a deep breath and drank in the wide expanse of farmland around me. I thought of how much easier such decisions were these days. I still struggled at times to keep my striving in check. But I had come a long way from where I was a few years earlier, when the very thought of making even small career sacrifices made me edgy. I marveled at how stealthily God works in the soul, one day and one trial at a time. He softens your edges so slowly and subtly that you can fail to notice how far you have come until you have moved on to the next problem. I wondered what other changes God might be working in my soul now, even as I saw no outward signs of progress at all.

Shivering as I realized that I had left my jacket in the car, I began strolling briskly toward the arched doors of the church. Surveying the building's beige, brick-and-limestone façade and the dim outlines of its stained-glass windows, I thought it looked a bit stark, even barren, against the austere rural landscape.

I changed my mind when I stepped inside. No sooner had I entered the sanctuary's warm embrace than I saw a trio of stained-glass windows towering before me, featuring three of my favorite saints. In the center was Teresa of Ávila, holding a tiny replica of one of the Carmelite monasteries she founded and a scroll with her signature line: "God alone suffices." To my right was Thérèse of Lisieux, standing amid roses and grasping an image of the suffering Christ beside a scroll bearing her famous words: "In the heart of the Church, we will be love." To my left stood Edith—Teresa Benedicta of the Cross—crowned by a halo of thorns and clutching a star of David and a scroll that said, "Love will be our eternal life."

Set aflame by the sunlight streaming through the window, the three silhouettes blazed in glory as if lit by God's love itself. Here were my heroines, my patronesses, my friends. Aside from Mary, the mother of Jesus, I could hardly think of three women I admired more. And the realization hit me with sudden force: Not one of them had borne biological children. Not one had been a mother in the conventional sense, the sense that I once thought I had to be a mother in order to "count" in the church and the world. Yet there they were, radiantly holy and beloved by countless spiritual children throughout the world, including me. Each had fulfilled, in her own way, what Edith described as the highest call of every mother: to nurture the spark of divine life in another's soul.

I realized as I gazed at the windows that the way these women looked to me now, from within the church, is how God saw them all the time. When he looked at these daughters of his, he saw beauty, not barrenness. He did not grieve their empty wombs. He celebrated their maternal hearts. He rejoiced that they had allowed him to use those hearts in his own mysterious ways.

I knew in that moment that God wanted to do the same with

me—that he could do the same, if I let him. He could make me a mother. He could even make me a saint. And he could do both without making me pregnant. He needed only my cooperation, my willingness to trade my own dreams and plans of motherhood for his.

I did not know if I could give him that. The pain of my childlessness still overwhelmed me at times. But I sensed that if I did, if I kept following, step by step, where he led, I could bear fruit beyond my imagining.

5

# Into the Darkness

In January 2008, on the twelfth anniversary of my father's Alzheimer's diagnosis, John and I stepped out under the gray skies of our suburban St. Louis neighborhood for a morning walk. The streets were clear and dry, but every corner we turned, bare trees and yellowed grass reminded me that winter was far from over.

"Dad's getting worse," I told John as our shoes crunched over salt crystals scattered during the last snowstorm. "He can barely walk more than a few feet now without resting. He's having trouble finding words. The other day, I couldn't get him to the bathroom in time and he had another accident in the hallway. I think he's in a new stage."

John nodded as I talked. He had noticed the changes himself. As a physician who recently had decided to specialize in geriatric medicine—a choice inspired largely by Dad—John knew as well as anyone what lay in store for a man with advanced Alzheimer's.

I knew, too. A few years earlier, I had found a chart online summarizing the seven stages of the disease. I scanned the symptom list for the first five stages—declining job performance, bungled finances, inappropriate clothing choices—and thought: *We can handle that; we've already handled that.* The sixth stage, which included occasional incontinence, gave me some pause. But it was the description of the seventh stage that chilled me. It said: "Speech ability declines to about a half-dozen intelligible words. Frequently there is no speech at all—only grunting. Incontinent of urine. Progressive loss of abilities to walk, sit up, smile and hold head up. The brain appears to no longer be able to tell the body what to do."

My eyes blurred with tears as I read those lines and pictured the drooling, glassy-eyed, wheelchair-bound dementia patients I had seen in my grandmother's nursing home. I quickly clicked my cursor over the chart and pasted it into a document that I did not intend to read again anytime soon. *Good God,* I had thought, *please don't let that happen to Dad.*

Not long after I discovered that list, in early 2006, Dad entered the sixth stage of Alzheimer's—and with it, a nursing home. The move pained my mother, who had juggled care for Dad with a full-time job for a decade before his needs finally overwhelmed her.

Dad's adjustment to institutional life was rough. He did not seem to know that he no longer lived at home—Mom's lengthy daily visits had convinced him that they still lived together—but he knew when the person bathing or dressing or toileting him was not his wife. It did not help that he was paired with a series of noisy roommates and a constantly changing cast of overworked, undertrained aides. Most of his caregivers seemed to mistake his dementia for deafness, shouting orders at Dad when he failed to follow spoken commands. Some barely talked to him at all, assuming, as I heard one mutter while leaving his room, that creating a pleasant environment for Dad "doesn't matter because he doesn't know where he is anyway."

Disoriented though he was, Dad suffered keenly from such slights. I would find him sitting at the nurses' station, desperately attempting to chat with aides who passed him in silence or grumbling about the "screwballs" who had ignored him all day. Once my mother found him alone in the dining room, holding his head in his hands and begging John Paul to send help from heaven. "I was confused and frightened," he told me a few minutes later. "I didn't know what was going on."

Mom and I considered moving Dad to another nursing home, but our other options seemed worse. So we devised a system to ensure that one of us always would be there to tuck him in at night and make sure his needs for food, exercise, and toileting were met before he went to bed. Usually it was Mom. At least once a week it was me.

Although my visits with Dad typically brought both of us joy, pulling into the nursing-home parking lot always filled me with anxiety. I never knew what I would find inside. It could be a good day, with Dad smiling and jolly, lurching forward to hug me as soon as I appeared. Or it could be a bad one, as when I found him alone and afraid in his room, urine-soaked pants around his ankles, pleading for help in plain sight of a hallway where dozens of aides had passed without stopping to help.

Such scenes were unfolding regularly by early 2008, which is what prompted me to unload my worries to John that January morning.

"I don't know what to pray for anymore when it comes to Dad," I said as I gazed up at the gnarled branches rustling angrily overhead. "Every week, it's more bad news. It's like the infertility. I feel like I'm living in limbo, always waiting for someone. I'm waiting for a baby or some doctor to tell us we can't have one, waiting for Dad to . . ."

I breathed deeply, wincing as the cold air stung my lungs.

"It's not like I want him to die," I said. "I just want his suffering to end. Or maybe I want my suffering to end. I feel like this is going to go on another twelve years."

John stared hard at the ground as we walked.

"He's not going to live another twelve years," he said.

"I know; it will probably only be a few more years, but—"

"He only has a year left."

I stopped and turned to John. My heart was pounding in my ears as his eyes met mine.

"What do you mean? Where did you hear that?"

"From your mom. She asked the doctor a few weeks ago how much time your dad had left, and the doctor said a year. Your mom wasn't sure it was true, so she didn't tell you."

"A year?" I felt an odd mixture of relief and panic as I repeated the words. "Only a year? But he's still so . . . so healthy. Do you believe that?"

"It's probably about right."

I suddenly remembered that this was my night to put Dad to bed. I had grumbled inwardly about it for the past several days, thinking I was too busy to deal with my demented father. Now I felt guilty and desperate to see him.

When I walked into his room that evening, I found Dad sitting with his hands folded as if he had been expecting me. He beckoned me to sit beside him. Between careful bites of the peanut-butter-and-jelly sandwich I had brought him, Dad shared what was on his mind.

"Sometimes we have to wait for people," he said in the hushed voice he reserved for his most important declarations. "But while we wait, we get better."

I felt a sudden surge of love and grief. Dad always seemed to know what I was struggling with, to know just what to say. I asked if he wanted to go for a walk with me.

"I want to go where God wants me to go."

We strolled slowly through the halls, and I snuck sideways glances at my father, trying to imagine him dying within a year. It seemed impossible. He always loomed so large in my eyes—that stocky frame, that barrel chest, those Popeye arms that propelled him to the Golden Gloves boxing championship in college. That was sixty years earlier, before old age and Alzheimer's. His arms looked skinnier now. His salt-and-pepper hair had turned all silver—when had that happened? He still cut an imposing figure sauntering down the hallway, though he stooped more than before. I felt something catch in my throat as I realized: He's slipping away.

We returned to his room, where I helped him to the bathroom and tucked him into bed. Dad stroked my hair and stared into my eyes for several moments, then pulled the covers tight to his chest.

"I love you," he said before squeezing his eyes shut and burrowing his head into the pillow like a baby.

On my way home, I stopped by Mom's apartment and offered to take her out for ice cream. After we settled into a booth at Dairy Queen and began munching on chocolate-dipped cones, I told her that John had informed me of Dad's one-year prognosis.

"Actually," she said, "the doctor thinks he has six months."

She looked down at her cone, then back into my eyes, now wide with disbelief.

"But she also said it could be a year."

## A Dark Road

Two weeks later I was awakened by an early-morning call from Mom. The charge nurse at Dad's nursing home was shipping him out to the emergency room on a stretcher—nude, we would later learn—because he had threatened an aide who tried to change him after a messy toileting mishap. Mom was on her way to the hospital. Did I want to meet her there?

Anxiety washed over me as I remembered the last time Dad had visited the emergency room, after a heart-attack scare four years earlier. Mom and I had taken turns waiting with him in the crowded ER for hours. The nurse who finally saw him drilled him with complex questions he could not possibly answer and shushed me each time I tried to explain his condition. The doctors insisted on admitting Dad to a regular cardiology floor for overnight monitoring despite Mom's concerns about his tendency toward agitation in strange settings and his need for skilled dementia care. Shortly after visiting hours ended, Dad awoke terrified and spent the rest of the night trying to escape the hospital and get home to Mom. The cardiology nurses, unaccustomed to handling advanced Alzheimer's patients, fought to reason with him and then restrain him in a nightmarish scene that left him ghostly pale and still breathing in the staccato style of a scared child when Mom arrived the next morning.

The prospect of another hospital visit with Dad filled me with dread. I wanted to comfort him, to reprise my role as the strong daughter who makes everything better for my mother and him. Yet the mere thought of walking into the ER and finding Dad nude and delirious made my heart race and my head pound. So I asked John to meet Mom there instead. Better to have a physician on hand than someone as squeamish as me, I told myself as I sheepishly handed him the phone. Besides, I had only one day left to pack for back-to-back business trips to Florida and Rome, trips on which John would accompany me. There was no way I could cancel them. One was a high-profile speaking engagement that I had planned for nearly a year, the first of a full slate of such events scheduled for the coming months. The other was the opportunity of a lifetime: a chance to serve as one of 250 delegates from around the world at a Vatican Congress on women, complete with a private audience with Pope Benedict XVI.

While I raced around St. Louis running errands that day, John kept me informed by phone of my father's progress. Dad had arrived at the hospital frightened and upset, and when the doctors tried to stick a needle into his veins to sedate him, he thrashed violently. Between shots, he cracked jokes and tried to charm the staff, probably hoping to distract them from what must have seemed to Dad to be a bizarre and unprovoked assault. The needles kept coming, though, and Dad kept resisting. It took six security guards to hold him down. The multiple doses of sedatives finally overpowered him, and Dad collapsed in exhaustion. When I arrived at the geriatric psychiatry ward late that afternoon, he was snoring as loudly as a bear. I felt guilty about having missed the drama but secretly grateful, too.

John and I set out the next morning on our trips. They were a whirlwind, and our time in Italy brimmed with unforgettable experiences. We met and chatted with Pope Benedict at his Ash Wednesday audience, shook his hand again at Mass that evening, and saw him in person again a few days later in the colorfully ornate Clementine Hall of the papal palace, where he addressed my women's conference. Benedict's gentleness, humility, and strong affirmation of women's gifts impressed me. So did the dozens of bright, fascinating, faithful Catholic women I encountered from regions as far-flung as Southeast Asia and sub-Saharan Africa. When the conference ended, John and I enjoyed an insider's tour of the Eternal City's churches with a Rome-based Jesuit friend from my Marquette days. He led us in prayers for my father and for a baby at the shrines of one heroic woman saint after another. The whole trip felt like a dream.

As soon as our plane touched down in St. Louis, though, the clouds descended again. I visited Dad in the psych ward and found him staring blankly from a wheelchair. I wished him a Happy Valentine's Day and waved the flowers I had brought for him under his nose. He did not answer. Nor did he respond when I hugged him and whispered my name in his ear. I knelt down before him and searched his eyes for some sign of recognition. I saw nothing. It was like talking to a cadaver.

Driving home that afternoon, I felt heartsick. Had I abandoned Dad in his time of need? Would I ever hear his voice again? I spent the next two days sending up frantic prayers and receiving regular updates from Mom while immersing myself in long-neglected desk work—an attempt to distract myself from the disaster unfolding with Dad. On the third day, I returned to the ward and found him in the same spot. This time, when I knelt down before his wheelchair and looked into his eyes, Dad looked back into mine and began chattering enthusiastically. His jovial prattle made no sense but sounded beautiful all the same. I began to weep right there, in full view of the nurses' station. An aide passed by and stole a curious glance at me as I rested my head on Dad's lap. I stifled a giggle, imagining how crazy the two of us must have looked—him babbling and me blubbering. I didn't care. I had my daddy back, at least for a little while. I had a little more time.

As I drove home that afternoon into a blazing pink sunset, I realized that Dad finally had entered the last stage of his disease, the one I had been dreading since he was diagnosed. The bad days would outnumber the good ones from now on, and the good ones would not be as good as they had once been. Dad's chipper personality could not shield him from what lay ahead, any more than the constantly changing scenery of my travel schedule could erase the grim reality I faced each time I returned home. I felt as if I were standing along the road to Calvary, watching my father stumble up the mountainside toward a final agony that I did not want to watch but knew I must.

## Redemptive Suffering

If I had to choose one element of the Catholic faith that Dad emphasized more than any other as I was growing up, it might be this: the belief that God does not abandon us in our suffering but uses suffering to draw us closer to him.

This concept is central to the biblical story. The Genesis creation accounts depict suffering not as part of God's original plan for humanity but as a consequence of the misuse of human freedom by our first parents, whose fall allowed sin and death to enter the world. Out of this "happy fault," as Saint Augustine called it, God brought a greater good: the Incarnation of his son, who redeemed us through his passion, death, and resurrection. God still allows evil in the world as the price of our freedom. Yet through his suffering, Christ transformed our trials into a means of grace, a way that we can participate in his redemptive work on earth while awaiting eternal life with him in heaven.

Allusions to the purifying and redemptive potential of suffering surface throughout the Hebrew scriptures. The book of Wisdom describes the "souls of the righteous" who "will shine forth" like "sparks through the stubble" because "God tested them and found them worthy of himself; like gold in the furnace he tried them, and like a sacrificial burnt offering he accepted them" (Wis. 3:1, 5–7). In Sirach, those who want to serve the Lord are warned to "prepare yourself for trials" because God tests "worthy men in the crucible of humiliation," and for those who remain faithful, "your reward will not be lost" (Sir. 2:1, 5, 8). Those verses are favorites at funeral masses because they echo Catholic belief in purgatory—a state of suffering in which imperfect souls who die in God's grace experience the purification after death that they did not complete during their earthly lives, so they can enter full union with the all-pure, all-holy God in heaven.

In the New Testament, Jesus alludes to the mystery of redemptive suffering repeatedly. He tells his disciples that "whoever does not take up the cross and follow me is not worthy of me" (Matt. 10:38) and explains his coming trials, and those of his followers, by reminding them that "unless a grain of wheat falls into the earth and dies, it remains just a single grain; but if it dies, it bears much fruit" (John 12:24). Saint Paul picks up this theme and weaves it through nearly all of his letters, urging his readers to "join with me in suffering for the Gospel" (2 Tim. 1:8) and reminding them that eternal joy awaits those who suffer with and for their Savior: "We suffer with him so that we may also be glorified with him. I consider that the sufferings of this present time are as nothing compared with the glory to be revealed to us. . . . For I am convinced that neither death, nor life, nor angels, nor rulers, nor things present, nor things to come, nor powers, nor height, nor depth, nor anything else in all creation, will be able to separate us from the love of God in Christ Jesus our Lord" (Rom. 8:17–18, 38–39).

I knew those verses well growing up, because they were among my father's favorites. He would read and reread Paul's words, quoting them to me amid the ups and downs of daily life after meditating on them in the mornings, along with the psalms he prayed daily in his breviary.

The only other book I saw captivate Dad as consistently as scripture was his tattered, coffee-stained copy of *The Collected Works of St. John of the Cross*. He carried it everywhere: to the den, his office, the Eucharistic adoration chapel, on our vacations and cross-country moves. He pored over its pages, highlighting their sentences, scrawling notes in their margins, and taping them back into place each time the book's exhausted spine threatened to collapse. Dad read that book for decades, until the fog of Alzheimer's forced him to stop.

I first read the writings of this sixteenth-century Carmelite priest and friend of Teresa of Ávila at age twenty-two. Flush with a new convert's enthusiasm and unnerved by the thought that my beginner's spiritual highs would not last forever, I quickly tucked them out of sight. I rediscovered John of the Cross a decade later, while sorting through Dad's books after he had moved to the nursing home. Thumbing through his favorite, dog-eared old tome, I came upon one section that was particularly marked up. In it, John said that just as Jesus achieved his greatest saving work through his sacrifice on the cross, amid feelings of abandonment by his heavenly father, so a follower of Jesus reaches the greatest degree of union with God when he is "brought to nothing" and thoroughly humbled. Few Christians are willing to enter into "this supreme nakedness and emptiness of spirit" that comes on the path toward union with Christ, John said. Upon taking their first taste of interior desolation, most "run from it as from death" and go back to trying to indulge their "spiritual sweet tooth." John writes, "From my observations Christ is to a great extent unknown by those who consider themselves his friends. Because of their extreme self-love they go about seeking in him their own consolations and satisfactions. But they do not seek, out of great love for him, his bitter trials and deaths."

Dad had drawn a black box around this section, then wrote beside it: "Perhaps the key to this whole book. When will I buy John's doctrine?" He penned those words around 1990, judging from the dates scribbled nearby. That was six years before he began his descent into dementia, before he became enveloped in a cognitive darkness that most of the world regards as senseless suffering. Yet Dad saw meaning in his trial. He had made that clear from the start. Reading that passage helped me understand why.

It also gave me a framework to understand another book that landed on my desk shortly before Dad landed in the hospital, one whose author would become a light to me as I struggled to make sense of Dad's suffering—and my own.

## A Saint of Darkness

"If I ever become a saint," Blessed Mother Teresa of Calcutta once wrote to a spiritual director, "I will surely be one of 'darkness.' I will continually be absent from heaven—to light the light of those in darkness on earth."

I first read that curious mission statement in late 2007, on the dust jacket of *Mother Teresa: Come Be My Light: The Private Writings of the Saint of Calcutta.* At the time, I was preparing to emcee an internationally televised conference on Mother Teresa's legacy, and the book's editor, Missionaries of Charity priest Father Brian Kolodiejchuk, was among those I planned to interview on-screen.

Father Brian, who was also tasked with promoting Mother Teresa's cause for canonization, was very much in demand that fall. That was due to the startling contents of his book, a never-before-published collection of Mother Teresa's private letters to her spiritual directors, which she had asked them to destroy. *Mother Teresa: Come Be My Light* had launched a global media frenzy with its revelation that the perpetually smiling "saint of the gutters" spent decades feeling abandoned by God.

Although word of Mother Teresa's spiritual struggles had leaked years earlier in the Catholic media, publication of her agonized letters shocked millions. Atheists blasted her as a pious fraud. Psychologists and psychiatrists labeled her a clinical depressive with masochistic tendencies. Journalists puzzled that the woman who publicly reminded others of God's unconditional love privately had written words like these: "When I try to raise my thoughts to Heaven—there is such convicting emptiness that those very thoughts return like sharp knives & hurt my very soul.—Love — the word—it brings nothing. — I am told God loves me—and yet the reality of darkness & coldness & emptiness is so great that nothing touches my soul. Before the work started — there was so much union — love—faith — trust — prayer — sacrifice. — Did I make a mistake in surrendering blindly to the call of the Sacred Heart?"

Like nearly everyone who admired Mother Teresa, I once had assumed that her interior life consisted of rapturous, soul-swelling prayer. How else could this diminutive religious sister find the strength to accomplish all she had in her eighty-seven years: to leave her Albanian home at age eighteen and join an Irish religious order that stationed her halfway around the world in India, to leave the comfort of her convent at age thirty-seven and launch a one-woman ministry to the dying and destitute in Calcutta's slums, to attract a following that eventually became the Missionaries of Charity, a worldwide community whose priestly, religious, and lay members now carry on her work in 133 countries? Mother Teresa won every honor from the Nobel Peace Prize to the U.S. Congressional Gold Medal and was beatified by the Catholic Church a mere six years after her death. She spent her days bathing AIDS orphans, emptying bedpans of homeless men, and picking maggots out of lepers' wounds, smiling all the while. She was the very picture of serene if unattainable sanctity. Surely, her spiritual life had brimmed with consolations.

Discovering that it was riddled with desolation instead did not shake my confidence that Mother Teresa was a holy woman. Her deeds alone manifested the sort of sanctity you cannot fake. Nor did I agree with secular pundits who cited Mother Teresa's letters as proof that she was just another garden-variety skeptic. I had read enough mystical theology to know that the interior trial of a woman passionately committed to Jesus is not the same as that of a casual seeker who cannot decide if God is worth her time.

Mother Teresa's darkness sounded to me much more like the "dark night of the soul" described by John of the Cross, who first coined the term. The phrase has devolved into a cliché in our culture, used to describe everything from slight spiritual hunger to a bout with the blues. But "the mystical doctor," as John is known, used it to describe a specific set of spiritual trials that God allows in the souls of those who love him so they can learn to love him more.

John of the Cross saw the spiritual life as a gradual and often painful process of letting go of all that is not God. Souls already purged of obvious sins may find God leading them through four increasingly intense "nights" to purify them of hidden sins and attachments and bring them into closer union with himself. The most trying of these is the "passive dark night of the spirit," John said, in which faith feels like a mirage and God feels absent, though he is closer than ever. Souls passing through this dark night feel the desolation that consumed Jesus when he cried out from the cross: "My God, my God, why have you abandoned me?" (Mark 15:34).

True dark nights of the spirit are rare, but periods of desolation and suffering are par for the spiritual course. When they are not merely the result of sinfulness or inattentiveness to God, John writes, these "darkness" experiences can lead to greater reliance on God, deeper contemplation, and clearer prioritizing of the things of God over the things of the world. At their pinnacle, he writes, they lead to a state of "transforming union" or "spiritual marriage," in which one feels God's presence almost all the time and trials seem less like a punishment than a grace, an opportunity to share in the redemptive suffering of Jesus. Many people quit or become stalled before they reach that point, however, frustrated at the loss of the pleasant spiritual feelings and external rewards that first attracted them to following Christ.

Mother Teresa was no quitter. Nor did she shrink from suffering, which her Catholic faith had taught her to view through the prism of Christ's passion. As a young nun, she had resolved to "drink the chalice [of the crucified Christ] to the last drop." She encouraged her sisters to do the same and to see their ministry to the suffering as means of meeting God in the flesh. As she explained once, "We may be doing social work in the eyes of the people, but we are really contemplatives in the heart of the world. For we are touching the body of Christ 24 hours." Mother Teresa counseled her sisters to find strength in prayer and the sacraments, especially the Eucharist, so they could recognize Jesus in the suffering souls they encountered daily.

Mother Teresa's steadfast prayer life and confidence in the reality of redemptive suffering allowed her to confront her own interior darkness armed with the conviction that her pain could glorify God. That conviction did not erase her pain, however, as the anguished tone of her private letters attests.

I read only snatches of those letters before emceeing the conference. I told myself that I was too busy to read more. In truth,

I was too spooked. What little I had read had unnerved me, just as John of the Cross's writings had a decade earlier. If someone as saintly as Mother Teresa felt forsaken by God and overwhelmed by her suffering, what hope was there for the rest of us? In my interview with Father Brian during the conference, I posed that question to him.

"A believer is watching this show," I said, "trying to grow closer to Christ and thinking: Okay, so what if I were to achieve the heights and do everything I can for God. Is this what I have to look forward to? Because it seems, frankly, reading her letters, kind of terrifying."

Father Brian paused, his rumpled gray shirt blending into a charcoal sketch of Mother Teresa displayed behind him.

"The closer you get, the more you're going to be suffering," he answered. "But the focus is not on the suffering. The focus and the important thing is the love with which that suffering is accepted and lived. And that's what really shows through all of these letters, is Mother Teresa's heroic faith . . . and just a real heroic love, which tells us that . . . as important as it is to feel love, in the end, love is not in feelings. It's in the will: in what I do, how I act, and what I choose. And Mother Teresa is a great example for reminding us and teaching us, once more, what love is."

Father Brian's answer had the ring of truth. It echoed similar answers my father had given me all my life. But only after I had watched Dad drink his own chalice to the last drop would I appreciate the light that Mother Teresa's example could cast into my own darkness.

## A New Crisis

Dad spent more than a month in the geriatric psychiatry ward before recovering enough of his appetite and alertness to return to nursing-home life. The director of his original home declined to take him back, so Mom scrambled to find another institution not intimidated by a burly, demented former boxer whose last home had booted him. She did not have the cash needed for a private-pay bed, and all the institutions with open Medicaid beds were rejecting Dad. The hospital social worker finally found one willing to take him: a modest, sunny little center not far from Mom's apartment. The place had a few blotches on its state inspection record, and the current resident of the room Dad would share had frequent seizures and a habit of keeping his television on full volume all night. After hearing the center's friendly director explain how her low patient population was a perk for residents, though, we thought maybe it could work. So we moved Dad in and hoped for the best.

A few days later, John and I were driving to meet a friend for dinner when I got a sinking feeling in my stomach.

"I think maybe we should visit Dad," I said.

"I do, too," John answered, surprising me by how quickly he turned the car in the direction of Dad's new home.

We arrived fifteen minutes later to find Dad sitting in a wheelchair at the nurses' station. I spotted new bruises on his arms. Two tattooed, gold-toothed aides sporting street clothes and shocks of pink hair were wrestling a jacket onto Dad, hollering at him as they forced his arms into the sleeves. He looked tired and scared, and I could tell from his greasy hair that he had not been bathed since he arrived. I asked the charge nurse what was going on.

"We're sending him out," she snapped, not bothering to glance up from her paperwork. "He threw some silverware at the dinner table."

I felt myself panicking, wondering how we could prevent another emergency-room visit. John introduced himself as a physician and asked the nurse to connect him with the house doctor. She shook her shaggy blond hair, curled her lip to reveal only one front tooth, then explained that the doctor already had approved Dad's transfer, despite never having visited her new patient or prescribed him the medication he needed for his behavioral and sleep issues. Dad watched the exchange anxiously, and when John took me aside to say that we should get my father out of this place right away, I agreed. The paramedics arrived a few minutes later. Dad surprised me by eagerly accepting their invitation to climb aboard the stretcher that he usually balked at riding. "Let's get going," he whispered, squeezing my hand. "Let's get out of here."

I rode in the ambulance with Dad, singing Irish songs to keep him calm while silently praying that his third ER visit would prove less traumatic than the first two. It was not to be.

Dad was whisked away as soon as we arrived, this time with John by his side, while Mom and I waited in the lobby. An hour after his arrival, the doctors waved us in to visit Dad on his ER cot. We found him lying in a faded hospital gown that barely covered his large frame, looking wan and defeated. Every few minutes he nodded off briefly, only to awaken in a bolt of terror and swing his legs off the side of the cot as if fleeing some invisible tormenter. In the harsh fluorescent light, I could see that the bruises I had glimpsed in the nursing home were more numerous than I had realized. When a nurse approached to give Dad a sponge bath and clean his groin area, he recoiled in fear, then cried out softly as she scrubbed him: "It's inhuman . . . It's murder . . . It's a sin." Mom and I tried to comfort him, and he would return our smiles and caresses for a few moments before nodding off and repeating the cycle of waking terror all over again. He was so confused, so jittery, so afraid—and so much worse than he had been four days earlier, when we had moved him into what I now recognized was an abusive nursing home.

The next day, John and I agreed that we needed to spend whatever it took to get Dad into a decent home. When I called Mom to say so, she said my brother had told her the same thing. So we all pooled our resources to secure a private-pay, single room in a nursing home that specialized in Alzheimer's care, one willing to take Dad if his family could make monthly cash payments in full. The home cost an exorbitant sum even split three ways. Between our own medical expenses, John's school loans, our hopes to buy a house sometime soon, and John's plans to pursue a low-paying geriatric fellowship that would delay the arrival of his full physician's salary for another year, I was not sure how long we could keep up our end of the payments or what would be left of our finances if we did. There was no question what Dad would do if the roles were reversed, though: He would take care of me and trust God to take care of him. I decided to do the same.

Dad's new home was shiny and beautiful, with more plentiful staff, dementia-appropriate activities, and an entire wing dedicated to late-stage Alzheimer's patients. On his first night there, John and I wheeled him over to the main dining room to see a South Pacific–themed musical revue. He was sleepy at first but soon perked up when he heard "Over the Rainbow." I did, too: That song had taken on special meaning for me since I heard Israel Kamakawiwo'ole's ukulele medley of it while celebrating John's medical-school graduation with a Hawaiian vacation. That was back in May 2005, when a baby still seemed to be just around the corner and Dad's nursing-home woes were nowhere in sight. Seeing rainbows on every island we visited and hearing that song up and down the radio dial, we had felt as if we were not far from that sweet spot where all our dreams would come true.

The meaning of that song had changed for me in the last three years. Lately, every time my iPod randomly clicked over to it, the tune prompted bitter tears about broken dreams. Not this time, though. As I watched my father whistle along with the singers, I thanked God for this brief break in the clouds. The man who had been on the brink of collapse a few days earlier had come back to life yet again. Dad clapped with me when the song ended, then leaned over and whispered in my ear: "God's mercy."

## Until Heaven

Dad enjoyed a fairly serene spring in his new nursing home. The aides there seemed less bewildered by his dementia. Mom and I relished the chance to spend our visits enjoying his company rather than doing the basic care tasks neglected by staffers in his last two homes.

Still, he was getting worse. He slept more and spoke less. When I dropped in to feed him lunch, he took fewer bites of his puréed food and frequently looked confused when it came time to swallow. His fingers often fidgeted and his hands moved in grand, sweeping strokes, as if he were conducting an imaginary orchestra. I gave him a colorful, oversized children's rosary, and he took to clutching it like a security blanket. I knew Dad still knew me by the way he opened his arms when he noticed me standing before him. Unfortunately, that moment of recognition took longer to happen now, as his gaze often seemed fixed on a faraway point.

"I want to go to heaven," he said when I found him whispering prayers with his hands folded on Easter Sunday.

Dad was hardly speaking at all by May 26, when I invited my mother and brother and his family to join John and me in celebrating my father's seventy-ninth birthday and my parents' thirty-eighth wedding anniversary. It had been too long since we all had gathered for a happy occasion, and I knew this might be our last with Dad. So I baked his favorite German chocolate cake and decorated his nursing-home room with fresh flowers and balloons. My niece and nephews jostled for spots on Grandma's lap, while John videotaped their antics and Tom and I reminisced about our childhood adventures with Dad. He smiled occasionally as if he got our jokes and ate some spoonfuls of cake I fed him, then slept through the rest of his soirée.

Two weeks later, as I was driving down the highway on my way to run an errand, the thought popped into my head: *I should see Dad.* I immediately resisted. I already had paid him several visits that week; I had a full slate of deadlines to meet; and I didn't feel up to the challenge of engaging him that day. Then I thought of all the other times I had paid attention to such inspirations and been glad I did. I veered right just in time to catch the exit for Dad's nursing home and arrived in his room a few minutes later.

Dad recognized me immediately. We embraced and he gazed

at me for a long time, silently stroking my face with his hands. He raised his arms to the sky, then lowered them back to me. He repeated the gesture several times with increasing urgency, as if trying to tell me something. His mouth was wide open in a smile full of wonder, but he did not speak. He looked beatific despite his gaunt cheeks. His skin glowed with a radiance I had not seen before. I began to talk to him, telling him everything I wanted him to know before he died.

"I love you, Dad," I said, tears streaming down my cheeks as I rested my palms on his large, soft hands, which now were cradling my face. "You've been a wonderful father to me. And now you're going home to heaven, home to Jesus. I'm going to miss you, but I'll be okay. It's okay for you to go."

His eyes grew brighter when I mentioned heaven, and he began gesturing again toward the sky.

"I know, Dad, I know. We're going to see each other again in heaven. And I know you'll be watching over me. I'll pray for you when you're gone, but I know you're going to heaven."

I leaned in close and looked deep into his eyes.

"Dad, when you get to heaven, will you do something for me? Will you ask Jesus to send me a baby?"

He smiled, his arms opening wider than ever.

"I love you, Daddy," I whispered as I nuzzled my head in his chest and wept. "I love you so much."

We spent three hours that way, Dad gesturing and me talking. I had not seen him stay awake that long in months, and though I felt reluctant to leave him, I wanted to go before he fell back into confusion or slumber. I wanted to seal that memory of him forever in my mind. I wheeled him down the hallway near the activity room and hugged him good-bye. As I turned to take a final peek at him over my shoulder, I saw him still looking longingly at me. So I walked back down the hall and knelt down beside him.

His blue eyes brimmed with tears as I gave him one last kiss. He smiled, opened his arms wide, and managed one parting word for me: "Joy!"

## Weeping with Jesus

Five days later, my brother walked into Dad's room and found him facedown on the floor beside his bed, struggling to pull himself up after a fall that apparently had gone unnoticed by the nursing-home aides for at least a half hour. That same day, a Catholic hospice house called Mom to inform her of a long-awaited opening, so they moved Dad there immediately.

I visited the next evening and found Dad in a deep sleep. Three days later, on June 19, he still had not awakened. The doctor said he was comatose and actively dying. My mother, brother, sister-in-law, John, and I held vigil at his bedside, caressing his skin, praying the rosary and the Divine Mercy chaplet for him, and whispering our teary good-byes in his ears. I told Dad the one thing I had forgotten to tell him earlier: that I was sorry for all the times I had failed to appreciate him, especially during my high school and college years.

Dad received last rites that afternoon, and by evening his labored breathing had become irregular and raspy. He still somehow managed to pucker his lips each time my mother asked for a kiss, however. At one point, when they were alone, he reached out in a brief bolt of determination and embraced her.

At 10 P.M., with Mom cradling his head and my brother and me holding his hands with our spouses at our sides, Dad drew a loud, exhausted breath. The air rattled his chest and his cracked lips as it rushed in. We waited for his exhale, but it never came.

Dad was dead. His great, good soul was gone. Within minutes, his deserted body looked luminous and wrinkle-free, as if already preparing for a glorious reunion with his spirit.

I sent John ahead to our home while I followed Mom back to her apartment in a separate car. Then I drove home alone through the thick darkness, down the same highway I had driven hundreds of times to see Dad at his apartment, his day-care center, his nursing homes and hospitals, and, finally, his hospice house. I thought of how odd it was that I would never drive that road again to see Dad, not ever. I could not comprehend the thought. It seemed like a mental game I was playing with myself, one of those crazy notions that I used to turn over in my mind late at night as a little girl, while sitting in the backseat on a family road trip, stargazing when I was supposed to be sleeping. On those nights, my mother and brother would be snoozing and my father would be trying to drive another hundred miles before he caved to exhaustion and pulled over to rent a motel room. He would catch my eye in the rearview mirror and wink, smiling because he knew I loved the dark stillness as much as he did.

Now there would be no more winks, no more songs, no more hugs. There would be no more Dad—at least, not the way I had known him—this side of eternity.

I believed Dad's suffering was over, and though I intended to pray dutifully for his soul, I believed he already had suffered his purgatory on earth, during his agonizing bout with Alzheimer's. I felt oddly light as I pondered the thought of Dad in heaven, seeing me tonight more clearly than he had in years, more clearly than ever before.

The sky cracked open above me, unleashing a fierce summer storm. As the raindrops pounded my windshield, I thought about Dad's body back in that hospice house. His soul had animated him, yes, and his soul was with God. But what of that big, cuddly body—the one that had consoled and embraced me for thirty-three years, even as his mind was deteriorating? It seemed scandalous that now it just sat deserted in that darkened room, awaiting a lonely ride to the morgue.

Sheets of water began striking my car, and I struggled to see the road. I swerved to the shoulder and parked beneath an overpass to wait for the rain to subside. I thought of that story in the Gospel where Jesus is told that his friend Lazarus has died. "He wept," it says, in a line that always puzzled me. Why would Jesus—the all-powerful, all-knowing Savior who conquered death by his resurrection—weep? And why would he weep just moments before raising Lazarus from the dead?

Remembering how Dad's broken-down body had strained violently for every breath at the end, I finally understood. Jesus wept because death is a horror—every death, even the death of a good man, even the death of someone on his way back to God. Jesus wept because death, like Alzheimer's and infertility, was never what he wanted for us. It was not part of God's original plan. Jesus saved us from death's finality; he brings greater good out of its pain; but death still horrifies us because that's the very nature of death: horrifying.

I watched the water cascading down the overpass before and behind me and imagined Jesus weeping with me over my loss, even as he embraced Dad in his merciful arms. When the pounding sheets lightened to a drizzle, I pulled back out onto the highway and headed home, eager to get some long overdue sleep and not quite sure what life would be like when I awoke.

## Feeling Blank

The next day the mysterious lightness of spirit I had felt in the wake of Dad's death disappeared. In its place came an oppressive mixture of sorrow and dread. I had told John to go to work as usual, to save his vacation days for the wake and funeral next week. I regretted doing so as soon as I heard our front door close behind him. There I was, surrounded by silence, trying to summon the energy to write a funeral notice and call friends I had not talked to in months or years to tell them that my father was dead. I would meet with my mother and brother to discuss funeral arrangements later that day, but I knew the three of us soon would return to our respective corners to nurse our grief in private. The loss of Dad had destabilized everything, and it seemed too deep to share.

We held Dad's wake five days later. As John and I pulled up to the funeral home, I silently prayed that despite Dad having suffered a dozen years from such an isolating disease, someone would come to bid him farewell. Four hours later, some two hundred people had passed his casket to pay their respects. Many were old friends, but many others had met Dad during his Alzheimer's years. They pulled me aside to share teary reminiscences of the jovial Irishman whose songs, blessings, and whispered reminders of God's love had lifted their spirits in crucial moments.

Another robust crowd filled the church the next day for a

funeral Mass concelebrated by five priests, at the conclusion of which my brother and I offered brief tributes to Dad. While greeting mourners outside the church afterward, I suddenly found myself swarmed by mini Mother Teresas. Draped in blue-and-white saris and standing no taller than their tiny foundress, this gaggle of beaming Missionaries of Charity took turns embracing me and telling me how much they had appreciated my remarks about Dad. Then they disappeared into the crowd as quickly as they had come. When I asked Mom about them later, she said their presence had surprised her because she knew only one or two of them through friends in the local lay branch of Mother Teresa's order. I felt as if the sisters were a heaven-sent sign, as if Mother Teresa herself wanted me to know that she was with me on the day I buried my father.

The burial was tough. The angry June sun was beating down on our little corner of the cemetery by late morning, and the air inside the burial tent was stifling. Tom and I sat on either side of Mom, holding her hands as the priest prayed before Dad's rose-covered casket. Beads of sweat disguised my tears as I listened to an Irish tenor sing "Danny Boy," Dad's favorite song, after the burial rite. I realized for the first time how melancholy it was, this tune that Dad had sung so many times to bring me joy. The ballad tells the story of a parent bidding farewell to a beloved child and asking that child to kneel and pray a graveside Hail Mary for the parent if death precedes their reunion. I stifled a sob when the crescendo came:

*And I shall hear, tho' soft you tread above me*
*And all my dreams will warm and sweeter be*

*If you will bend and tell me that you love me*
*And I will sleep in peace until you come to me.*

Burying Dad turned out to be easier than navigating the next few months. The crowds dispersed, the strangeness of Dad's death wore off, and a heavy pall settled over my life. I looked up after years of careening from crisis to crisis with my father and my infertility and realized that I had neglected friendships, failed to make time for almost anything other than work and family disasters, and reached a point of utter exhaustion in my grief over Dad and the baby I could not conceive.

Everywhere I turned, the world reminded me that death was merely part of the "circle of life," as one well-wisher put it to me. Your parents die; your children are born; life goes on. But there was no circle of life for me. For me, the circle stopped with Dad's death. I saw my brother holding tightly to his five children in the months after we lost Dad, but I had no children to hold. John and I had only each other. As much a comfort as John was to me, when I looked into our future, I once again saw that gaping black hole that had stretched out before me the morning we first learned of our infertility. I pictured myself losing John someday, then spending my final years in a lonely solitude unrelieved by visits from children or grandchildren. It did not help that every time I picked up the phone in the months after Dad's death, I seemed to be hearing from another old friend announcing her second or third pregnancy. I would choke out a cheery "Congratulations," ask all the right questions, then hang up and sit in silence. I would think about Dad's death and my own, wondering how much more frightening death must be when you face it alone.

The chaos of Dad's final decline had convinced John and me to shelve fertility treatments for most of 2008. When I turned thirty-four that September, I reflected dryly on the fact that my window for biological motherhood had all but closed. I always had considered thirty-five my fertility D-day: Either conceive by that age or give up. I felt too burnt out to endure more fertility treatments and too depleted to investigate adoption. It was as if all the grief and rage and disappointment of recent years had congealed into one cold, hard mass of apathy that I could not shake. I no longer knew what to look forward to, what to pray for, what to want. I felt blank. I wondered: What if all this suffering is pointless after all?

I still believed that God was good. And deep down, I believed that God had a plan for me, one in which my suffering made sense. What I began to doubt was that I would ever understand that plan or feel grateful for it in this life. God's goodness seemed like an abstract theory that I accepted but could not prove. As for heaven, I believed that Dad had gone there, and I wanted to join him someday. I just didn't know what to do with myself in the meantime. How would I persevere in the face of a trial that seemed endless and a future that looked lonely, boring, and bleak?

God gave me no answers. When I prayed, I felt as if I were talking to a wall. My career felt equally unrewarding. I was doing exactly the sort of work I had always wanted to do. Yet the more people complimented my op-ed columns, speeches, and television shows, and gushed about how my work had strengthened their faith, the more cheated and ashamed I felt by my distance from God. The spiritual books and saints' quotes that once had inspired me now wearied me. Even memories of Dad left me cold. I tucked away most of his photos and letters, fell silent when my mother and brother swapped memories of his good old days, and refused John's invitations to screen videos from his final years. I did not want to mourn him anymore, miss him anymore, see the bright side of his suffering anymore. I was sick and tired of all of it.

I knew I was teetering on the brink of a dangerous cliff. The only safe thing I knew to do was to keep showing up for daily Mass, keep reading scripture, keep confessing my sins, and keep visiting my parish's Eucharistic adoration chapel. I would sit in the back row of that chapel night after night, staring hard at the little white host in the monstrance. I knew Jesus was there. I believed in his Eucharistic presence as much as ever. But I felt none of the warm waves of consolation that used to come in his presence, only periodic flashes of despair about my future or irritation at my rosary-rattling, denture-clicking, page-rustling fellow adorers.

It was about this time that I finally dug out the book of Mother Teresa's private writings that Father Brian had inscribed for me a year earlier. Reading her letters in full for the first time, I was surprised to discover that this saint I once regarded as impossibly holy could speak so powerfully to the blackness suffocating my soul.

## Mother Teresa's Dark Night

In September 1946, while still an India-based sister in the teaching order of Our Lady of Loreto, thirty-six-year-old Mother Teresa took a lengthy train trip from Calcutta to Darjeeling. She received on that ride her "call within a call." A voice spoke to her in the first of what she described to her spiritual directors as a series of visions and interior locutions from Jesus. In them, Jesus invited her to leave all and "come be my light" in the slums of Calcutta. He wanted her to satiate the thirst he felt on the cross for love and for the salvation of souls by founding an order of sisters who would be both "Mary and Martha" in the lives of the poor, radiating God's love as they shared the poverty of those they served. Hesitating at first, Mother Teresa agreed when Jesus reminded her of a private vow she had made four years earlier to refuse him nothing, no matter what he asked.

Over the next year, as Mother Teresa lobbied church authorities for permission to begin her ministry, she experienced an intense union with Jesus that her spiritual director described to her archbishop as so "continual . . . deep and violent that rapture does not seem very far." Attracted to penance and longing to suffer extravagantly for love of Jesus, Mother Teresa continued to feel this intoxicating bliss of union through the start of her street ministry. Then, just as her most fruitful and challenging life's work was beginning, her sense of intimacy with Jesus evaporated. It was replaced, she later wrote, by "such terrible darkness within me, as if everything was dead."

For the first few years after this secret darkness descended, Mother Teresa chalked it up to her own sinfulness. She figured that her strong, stubborn personality required a particularly long and harsh purification. She sought advice from one spiritual director after another, agonized over the thought that she was doing something to keep Jesus away. She remained faithful to her rigorous schedule of prayer and service to the poor, edifying others with her joyful smiles, encouraging words, and hours of Eucharistic adoration. Inside, though, she suffered a searing pain, one all the more intense because she had experienced its opposite.

Mother Teresa enjoyed a brief respite from her pain in October 1958, when she asked God to send proof that he was pleased with the work she and her sisters were doing. "There & then disappeared that long darkness," Mother Teresa confided to her bishop. "Today my soul is filled with love with joy untold." The desolation soon returned, however, harsh as ever. Prompted by a confessor to pen a letter to Jesus the next year, she wrote that she felt the pain souls in hell must feel,

> that terrible pain of loss—of God not wanting me—of God not being God—of God not really existing (Jesus, please forgive my blasphemies—I have been told to write everything). That darkness that surrounds me on all sides—I can't lift my soul to God—no light or inspiration enters my soul.—I speak of love for souls—of tender love for God—words pass through my [lips]—and I long with a deep longing to believe in them.—What do I labor for? If there be no God—there can be no soul.—If there is no soul then Jesus—you also are not true.—Heaven, what emptiness—not a single thought of heaven enters my mind—for there is no hope.—I am afraid to write all those terrible things that pass in my soul.—They must hurt you.
>
> In my heart there is no faith—no love—no trust—there is so much pain—the pain of longing, the pain of not being wanted.—I want God with all the powers of my soul—and yet there between us—there is a terrible separation.—I don't pray any longer —I utter words of community prayers—and

> try my utmost to get out of every word the sweetness it has to give.—But my prayer of union is not there any longer.

A turning point came in 1961, nearly a dozen years into her trial. Mother Teresa confided in a new Jesuit spiritual director, Father Joseph Neuner. He told her that the desolation she felt was not her fault; it was a dark-night experience with no human remedy. This was no typical dark night, though, since Mother Teresa already had endured a purifying period of darkness before she reached the heights of mystical union years earlier. This was something different: a "reparatory" or "apostolic" darkness meant not to purge sin from the one who endures it but to allow that soul to suffer on behalf of others who do not love God as they should. Father Joseph urged Mother Teresa to accept this prolonged suffering as the spiritual side of her work, an opportunity to help satiate Jesus's thirst for love on the cross by sharing that thirst in her depths. As for her fears of God abandoning her, he said that the intense longing Mother Teresa felt for Jesus was a sure sign of God's hidden presence within her soul.

Father Joseph's advice elated Mother Teresa. She realized that her loving embrace of this trial could make her ministry more fruitful, by allowing her to feel the same abandonment and lack of love that Jesus felt on the cross. It could help her empathize more with those she served, both the materially poor and the emotionally and spiritually poor, whose feelings of "being unloved, unwanted and uncared for" she saw as the greatest poverty. As she wrote to Father Joseph, "For the first time in this 11 years—I have come to love the darkness.—For I believe now that it is a part, a very, very small part of Jesus's darkness & pain on earth. . . . Today really I felt a deep joy—that Jesus can't go anymore through the agony—but that he wants to go through it in me.—More than ever I surrender myself to him.—Yes—more than ever I will be at his disposal."

Glimpsing God's mysterious purposes at work in her trial did not numb its pain or make it disappear. Mother Teresa's letters suggest that her darkness remained with her for nearly five decades, until her death in 1997. Such a lengthy dark night is almost unheard of among the saints, though its reparative aspect—the fact that it seemed to be about suffering for the sake of others rather than purifying her own sins—has interesting parallels with Mother Teresa's namesake in religious life, Thérèse of Lisieux.

Thérèse, who made the same vow as Mother Teresa to refuse Jesus nothing, was plunged into what she described as "the thickest darkness" the last year and a half of her life. Her mind was invaded by temptations to despair and disbelief. An avid reader of John of the Cross, Thérèse recognized them as a trial allowed by God. When assaulted by such temptations, she said, "I run toward my Jesus. I tell Him . . . I am happy not to enjoy this beautiful heaven on this earth so that He will open it for all eternity to poor unbelievers."

Mother Teresa made similar acts of faith throughout her life, and her letters indicate that she drew occasional strength from the works of John of the Cross. The union with Jesus she once had lived in bliss she now consented to live in desolation, a mysterious answer to the desire she had expressed years earlier "to love Jesus as he has never been loved before" and to drink his "chalice of pain" to "the last drop." Like Saint Paul, who said, "I rejoice in my sufferings for your sake, and in my flesh I complete what is lacking in Christ's afflictions for the sake of his body, that is, the Church" (Col. 1:24), Mother Teresa embraced her pain for love of

Jesus and his church even before she understood its purpose. She made this clear in her 1959 letter to Jesus, the one she wrote while still stumped about the reason for her desolation:

> If my separation from you,—brings others to you and in their love and company you find joy and pleasure—why Jesus, I am willing with all my heart to suffer all that I suffer—not only now—but for all eternity—if this was possible. Your happiness is all that I want. . . . I want to satiate your thirst with every single drop of blood that you can find in me.—Don't allow me to do you wrong in any way—take from me the power of hurting you. . . . I beg of you only one thing—please do not take the trouble to return soon.—I am ready to wait for you for all eternity.

## A Simple Way

Reading those words, I was astonished by Mother Teresa's willingness to suffer for Jesus. It was a beautiful and fearsome thing to behold, this reckless passion she harbored for a God who appeared to have abandoned her. I could not help but be humbled by the vast chasm between the heroic, joyful way Mother Teresa had carried her cross and the halfhearted, resentful way I was carrying mine.

Mother Teresa's letters did not discourage me, though. Unlike just about everything else I read that fall, they inspired me. I knew that I was no Mother Teresa and my desolation was no dark night of the spirit. But her tortured missives helped me realize that I was experiencing shades of what mystics like John of the Cross describe as the darkness of faith: the challenge of clinging to Christ when it feels as if he has forgotten you. I wondered if Dad had wrestled with that same challenge during the first few years after his Alzheimer's diagnosis, when he still was lucid enough to know the terrors that awaited him and to remember how his own dementia-stricken mother had suffered in her final years. Perhaps his determination to lean on God amid the encroaching darkness explained that phrase he repeated like a mantra throughout his illness. "I'm in God's hands," he would tell me, whenever I asked how he was. "We're all in God's hands."

I had heard that phrase for years, along with its peculiarly Catholic corollaries: "offer it up," "carry your cross," "unite your sufferings with the suffering of Jesus." I always thought I knew what they meant: that we should trust God and offer up our suffering when facing such obvious trials as illnesses, difficult decisions, and the loss of loved ones. What I had never known or understood was what to do with the anguished uncertainty that accompanies such trials and the inchoate, interior suffering that often proves more daunting than external predicaments.

"I can accept the cross of never having children," I told my mother once. "It's the waiting, the not knowing, that's driving me crazy."

"The waiting *is* the cross," she answered.

Those words flew right past me when I first heard them. Now, reading Mother Teresa's anguished letters, they came back with a wallop. Maybe that was the truth I had overlooked all these years: that the waiting, the not knowing, even the interior desolation and doubts—*that* was the suffering that Jesus wanted me to offer up to him. Maybe the prayer Jesus wants in dark times is not one of petition or inquisition but one of simple surrender to the Father's will, the same prayer that Jesus himself offered from the cross.

I wanted to analyze and dissect my cross, to know how long I would have to carry it and how my carrying it would glorify God. Like a groggy patient fighting to sit upright amid her operation so she can monitor her surgeon's progress, I wanted to stand outside my suffering and scrutinize God's work in my soul as he accomplished it.

Jesus, I realized, wanted none of this. He did not need my supervision, and he was not asking me to understand my cross. He was asking me to carry it. He wanted me to wake up each morning, bend a knee on the cold wooden floor beside my bed, and offer that day's sufferings and joys for whatever purposes he wished to use them. He wanted me to joyfully embrace my daily duties and leave the big picture to him—to do, in other words, what Mother Teresa had done when facing much harsher trials than mine.

That style of one-foot-in-front-of-the-other spirituality had never much appealed to me. It seemed too simplistic for the deep-thinking Christian I considered myself to be. But day after day, as I soaked up Mother Teresa's words in that chapel and stared at that silent host, I grew in my conviction that such simple perseverance might just be the essence of authentic faith: showing up to pray when you feel nothing, continuing to confide in God when he answers you with silence, loving and serving him even after you accept that he may never give you what you so desperately want or answer the question that confounds you most. That was the blind faith that sustained Mother Teresa through her decades of desolation. It was the faith that sustained Dad through his crucible of dementia. And it was the faith Jesus was trying to teach me, through the very trials that I kept begging him to take away.

One phrase kept coming back to me as that fall faded into winter: God is God, and I am not. After years of pretending to believe that truth, I finally felt it sinking into my bones. I cannot control God. I cannot predict God. I cannot force God to do what I want or explain why he has not done what I want. I cannot manipulate him with my prayers or deeds or feigned resignation to his will. And the well-meaning people who challenge me to try—by assuring me that they just *know* God will give me a baby or they *know* exactly why God allowed my father to suffer dementia for a dozen years—are wrong. No one knows the ways of God, not fully. He is a merciful and loving father who works all things to the good for those who love him, yes. But he does not answer to me, or to any of us, for the mysterious ways he does his redeeming work. "For my thoughts are not your thoughts," scripture says, "and my ways are not your ways" (Isa. 55:8). In the face of such mystery, the only appropriate response is humble gratitude. It is the gratitude of a child who recognizes her utter dependence on God for every blessing and trusts that he will turn even her sorrows to joys—in a way and at a time of his choosing, not hers.

I was not that child, not yet. My recent trials and desolation had brought me closer to the mark than had the sunnier times of years past, however. I began to imagine the freedom that must come from living in constant gratitude to God, the sort of gratitude I saw in my father in his final years and in Mother Teresa her entire life. How liberating it must be to stop evading, questioning, or complaining about your trials and start embracing them as opportunities to draw closer to God, to realize that even if Jesus is all you have, he is enough.

## Sign of Hope

On the first day of 2009 John and I stepped off a cruise ship and onto the shores of Costa Maya, Mexico, a small tourist region still recovering from the ravages of Hurricane Dean, which had ripped through the area a year and a half earlier. The cruise was a splurge we had planned in the bleakest days of the fall as something to get us through my first Christmas without Dad and another holiday season without children. Upon arriving at our port of call, we rented a golf cart and set off in search of a Mass to attend on this Solemnity of Mary, the Mother of God, since it was a holy day of obligation and no Masses had been offered on the ship. We had little time—we were getting a late start and had to be back on the ship by five—but we were hoping to tour the region after Mass.

Our afternoon quickly devolved into a debacle. We took a series of wrong turns trying to locate the tiny, out-of-the-way chapel that functioned as the village's only church. We finally found it, only to discover that it was still boarded up from the hurricane. When we hopped back onto our golf cart for a quick getaway from this desolate part of the peninsula, the engine refused to start. Dark clouds began gathering overhead as we scanned the horizon and realized that the taxis so plentiful at the port and on the beach were not cruising side roads like this one.

After waiting and wandering for an hour, we managed to hail a cab. The driver dropped us back at our port of call, where we rented another golf cart and sped off once again. No sooner had we found the winding coastal road that led us to the most scenic views of the ocean than the clouds above us opened up, unleashing a blinding rainstorm that left us shivering and drenched, huddling for shelter under a scrawny, hurricane-twisted tree.

By the time the rain stopped, we had only an hour left before we needed to return to the ship. So we resigned ourselves to combing the touristy part of the beach we had hoped to avoid. I stopped to buy a few colorful ceramic tiles from a Mexican woman about my age, who was painting under a porch with her three little girls scampering underfoot. As she wrapped up the tiles for me, I gazed at those three beautiful children twirling around the porch posts and hovering near her skirt. This woman obviously was poorer than me, yet she had something I desperately wanted and could not have: children of her own. I felt that old familiar sorrow threatening to wash over me like the cold, wet T-shirt still soaking my chest and back.

Just then, I looked out at the shoreline and saw two full rainbows arched in the sky, framing the cruise ship that would take John and me home. Struck speechless by their beauty, I nudged John. I pointed out the rainbows first to him, then to the three little girls, who began poking their mother excitedly to show her the sight. She stopped her wrapping and smiled. For a few silent moments, the six of us simply stared in awe at God's handiwork.

Gazing at the brilliant colors and perfect roundness of those rainbows, I immediately thought of Dad, whose presence seemed palpable in that moment. I thought of the "Over the Rainbow" song that he and I had enjoyed together before he died and of the many rainbows that John and I had glimpsed together in Hawaii years earlier.

I began to think of all I still had to look forward to when John and I boarded that ship and headed back home. We had meaningful work to do, a comfortable place to lay our heads, and a marriage full of love. Even our parenthood forecast had a few bright spots. We recently had found a fertility specialist with a new take on our case and a willingness to work within the limits of our Catholic faith, including our refusal to pursue IVF. And I had just started talking with a new friend whose successful domestic-adoption story allayed some of my fears about adoption's legal hassles and about a birth mother reclaiming a child years down the road. Although John and I still sensed God calling us to try to conceive, we did not want to delay parenthood much longer. So we had resolved to spend two more months in early 2009 trying for a biological child, then turn our attention to adoption.

We also had made another new year's resolution: to pray the rosary together every day. This quiet, biblically based meditation on the life of Christ and his mother had served as a cornerstone spiritual practice for nearly every Catholic we admired, including my father and Mother Teresa. Now we wanted to experience its power in our lives, not just sporadically and on our own but as a family—which is what the two of us already were by virtue of our sacramental marriage.

I realized as I stood on that shoreline that the shadows dogging me since Dad's death had started to recede and left me changed in their wake. I felt freer and lighter, shorn of my weighty expectations and illusions of control. Taking the place of my desolation was not joy so much as the promise of joy. With Mother Teresa as a beacon, I had arrived at the conviction that I could find a way to be happy with whatever Jesus gave me, as long as I had him.

Something about those two perfectly formed rainbows before me—not just one, but two—reinforced that conviction. I felt as if God were sending me a reminder, perhaps at my father's request, that just as swiftly and lavishly as he had brought stunning beauty to the shores of this place so devastated by a natural disaster, he could bring beauty out of my devastation, too.

6

# Triumph of the Cross

I first heard the prayer as a pigtailed Catholic schoolgirl, and it immediately became my favorite. I did not know of its storied fifteenth-century origins or its status as a favorite of famed preacher and Doctor of the Church Saint Francis de Sales. I knew only that it sounded more exotic than the Our Father or Hail Mary and that it began by reminding the mother of Jesus of her track record for responsiveness—a savvy tactic for securing her help, I thought. Most important, I knew that the Memorare worked. Whenever I murmured this classic prayer for Mary's intercession, good things happened. Its power had so impressed me as a child that I had resolved not to pray it except in dire circumstances, lest I wear out its effectiveness.

Memories of childhood Memorare recitations returned to me one frigid Friday morning in late January 2009. I was driving home from a break-of-dawn blood draw at the hospital, listening absently to a CD from Catholic singer-songwriter Danielle Rose. My new doctor, a fertility specialist whose fresh approach and respect for our decision to refuse IVF had inspired us to give him a try, was a believer in lab-based pregnancy tests rather than home kits. That meant I would have to wait several hours for results that I was accustomed to receiving after only three minutes. I told myself I didn't mind, since I already knew the outcome. After forty-eight months of infertility, there was no mistaking the familiar flashes of moodiness and breast tenderness that told me my period, not a baby, was on the way.

While winding through the valley road that led back to my house, I heard the first plaintive notes of "Memorare," Danielle's musical version of my beloved childhood prayer. I resisted its poignant pull, determined to keep my emotions in check so I could shrug off the day's disappointment like a champ. I already had done my praying earlier in the month; conception had not occurred; now it was time to focus on the next steps that John and I would take to pursue parenthood another way. Although it was only the first month of the final two that we had given ourselves to conceive, I sensed that this was it, that for better or worse, our quest to become biological parents would end today.

As I listened to the Memorare's opening lines, they moved me in spite of myself. They seemed to spring from my own depths, from a little girl who still dreamed of a baby of her own and still believed that Jesus and his mother would send her one. I had asked so many times before, using this prayer and a thousand others. What was the point of asking again? Yet as the song unfolded, I felt an interior prodding to do just that, to put aside my pride and probabilities and ask, one more time, for a miracle. So I started to sing along with those familiar words:

*Remember, O most gracious Virgin Mary,*
*That never was it known*
*That anyone who fled to thy protection, implored thy help or sought thy intercession*
*Was left unaided.*
*Inspired by this confidence, I fly unto thee, O virgin of virgins, my mother.*
*To thee do I come, before thee I stand, sinful and sorrowful.*
*O mother of the Word Incarnate,*
*Despise not my petitions, but in thy mercy, hear and answer me.*

By the time the song ended, I was weeping.

"Please," I whispered as I smeared a palm across my tear-stained cheeks, "please, just once, let it be good news."

I returned home a few minutes later, gave my nose a good blow, and sequestered myself in my office without even pausing to take my morning shower. Flipping on my computer, I resolved to make the most of this writing day despite my brief outburst of baby drama.

I was so immersed in the revision of a tricky paragraph two hours later that I felt disoriented when my desk phone rang. Then I saw who was on the line. I sprinted to my bedroom to answer the call, hoping to quarantine the awful news there so it would not infect my work space. Gulping as much air as my lungs could hold, I reached for the receiver and reminded myself that closure is a good thing, even when it stings.

"Colleen," the nurse said, "I have good news for you."

My hand started to shake as I struggled to hold the receiver.

"You're pregnant."

"No."

"Yes, Colleen, you are."

"No, I can't be."

I felt a smile inching across my face, but I squelched it.

"There must be some mistake," I said, determined not to unleash years of pent-up hope on a medical error. "I've never been pregnant, not once. I've never even had a miscarriage. It must be a false positive. Are you sure it isn't a false positive?"

"I'm sure, Colleen," she said, chuckling. "You're definitely pregnant."

I felt light-headed as she explained that the pregnancy hormone levels in my blood were very high—too high for a misreading. I suggested that perhaps she had mixed up my lab report with someone else's. No, she said, these are your results, and you're pregnant. She quickly shared a few other details about follow-up tests and appointments. I did my best to respond appropriately, but the smile now cemented on my face made it tough to form sentences.

My hands were still shaky as I gingerly placed the phone back on its charger. Everything around my silent, beige bedroom seemed brighter and louder, pulsing with cosmic importance.

"Oh my God," I murmured, sinking to my knees and lifting my eyes to the crucifix I had stared at years earlier as I overheard

John discuss our infertility diagnosis for the first time. I thought of Elizabeth, cousin of Mary and mother of John the Baptist, who had thanked God for delivering her from her barrenness. Her words became my own.

"Oh my God, you delivered me. Jesus, you delivered me. Oh thank you, thank you, Jesus, for delivering me."

Tears streaked my face for the second time that morning. I laughed out loud, then covered my mouth with my hands and listened to my heart pounding in my ears, marveling that another heart was pounding within my womb. Why did Jesus do this for me? Why now, after all these years? Why me, when so many infertile women never get this call? I felt like a fickle lover, lavished with a gift so far beyond her merit and expectations that she can greet it only with embarrassed protestations of her unworthiness. I promised myself that no matter what happened from here on out, I would never forget my gratitude in this moment.

After several minutes on my knees, I scrambled to my feet, grabbed my car keys, and darted toward the front door. It was all I could do not to fly down the highway to the nursing home where John was seeing patients that morning. I tried to keep a straight face when he walked into the crowded lobby to meet me, but my megawatt grin burst through and gave me away.

"I'm pregnant," I whispered as he swept me into a fierce hug.

Curious strangers scrutinized us, probably wondering what that frenzied woman with a greasy ponytail and torn sweatpants had told that nice, clean-cut doctor. We scurried outside to indulge our joy in the privacy of the snow-packed parking lot, giggling like schoolchildren over the incomprehensibility of it all.

"There's someone in there," he said, reeling back from our embrace and pointing to my belly.

"I know," I said, my laughter mixing with shivers as we huddled in the cold. "Can you believe it?"

"No, I can't," John answered.

A cloud of frosty breath escaped his lips, which were now spread in a grin as massive as mine.

"Does it feel like a boy or a girl?"

"It doesn't feel like one or the other," I said.

And for a moment, I thought: It almost feels like both.

## A Shadow Falls

A few weeks later, while I was lying on the exam table for my first pregnancy ultrasound, John and I got the second-biggest surprise of our lives.

"There are two in there," the technician said coolly, her eyes locked on the fuzzy black-and-white screen to my right. "Now I need to see if they have heartbeats."

John and I gasped, then exchanged astonished smiles and clasped hands. I held my breath while the technician adjusted the probe within me.

"I have a heartbeat on Baby A," she said.

John squeezed my hand. The technician moved the probe again.

"I have a heartbeat on Baby B."

John let out a hushed cheer, and we embraced. The miracle of my pregnancy had just multiplied. I felt sure that my father had something to do with this newest twist: Twins were a big, bold gesture, the kind that Dad specialized in all his life. I could imagine him pumping his fist from heaven, telling me that after all my troubles, "you came out smelling like a rose."

The next few weeks were a blur of nausea, fatigue, and progesterone supplements designed to protect against miscarriage. We found an obstetrician who delivered at the hospital near our home, and I followed his advice to keep up my exercise and travel schedule as best I could, though my exhaustion some days made it difficult. My robust appetite disappeared, and sleep came earlier each night, along with hot flashes and mood swings that made PMS look like a cakewalk. I felt like hell, but I didn't mind. I was pregnant—with twins. Two little people were growing within me. How could I beat that?

John and I resolved to tell only a handful of loved ones about the pregnancy until we safely cleared the first trimester at the end of March. I did not want to celebrate publicly too soon, lest I wind up mourning a miscarriage before an audience. Every morning when I awoke, I ducked into the bathroom and checked for signs of a late-arriving period, exhaling when I found none. My confidence grew with each passing day. I felt as if I were hiding the biggest, best secret of my life within my still-flat belly.

One afternoon in early March, while John was out of town and I was home polishing a speech I needed to deliver at a pro-life benefit that night, I felt an odd wetness in my seat. I rushed into the bathroom and found bright red blood on my underwear. I gasped, my hands trembling as I pulled my pants back on and dialed my obstetrician's office. *This is it*, I thought. *I'm losing the babies.*

The nurse told me to come in immediately for an emergency ultrasound. Mom drove me, and we both stared in silence as the technician searched the screen for signs of life. She found my babies right away. They were larger than last time, and both hearts were beating. Baby A even made a waving motion across the forehead and chest, in what looked to me like a tiny sign of the cross.

Unfortunately, the technician also found something else on that ultrasound: an internal tear that had produced a small pocket of blood between the membranes of one of the placentas and the uterus. This subchorionic hemorrhage, as it later would be diagnosed, looked like only a slight and harmless shadow that day. But a week later I had another bleeding incident, and then another. The shadow was growing.

My obstetrician continued to counsel me to keep up my normal schedule. He said the bleeding probably was not serious and, in any case, would not be affected by anything I did. He brushed off my hypothesis that air travel seemed to exacerbate my condition, scolding me for being too eager to surrender my active lifestyle for my unborn babies. He was similarly dismissive of John's questions about whether I should stop taking the baby aspirin that another obstetrician had prescribed for me months earlier, as part of an experimental treatment to prevent the possibility of early, undetected miscarriages.

"Doesn't matter," our new obstetrician said every time John raised the issue of aspirin's anticlotting effects. "The dose is too low to be contributing to Colleen's bleeding. She should stay on it."

We followed his advice against our better instincts. I spent the rest of my first trimester popping my daily aspirin, taking vigorous morning walks, and hopping on and off planes, lugging my bags and books to speaking engagements across America. The bleeding incidents kept happening, and with each ultrasound the shadow loomed larger. By the time my obstetrician finally acknowledged that it was a severe problem he could neither explain nor treat, John and I were fed up with his casual approach and fearful for our babies' lives.

The rotating team of perinatal specialists we saw next confirmed our fears. They assigned me a series of biweekly ultrasounds and put me on partial bed rest. Although I abided strictly by their recommendations, things got worse with each new ultrasound. The babies were growing, but so was the bleed. There were now three separate bleeds in my womb, not just one. A large pocket of flowing blood was forming between the babies' placental sacs, threatening to invade their food supply and choke off their lives.

"It's going to be a nightmarish, harrowing pregnancy," one specialist told me after viewing my scan.

"If this keeps up," another said, "you're screwed."

The ultrasounds had their happy moments. With each one, John and I saw more of the squirming, flipping, thumb-sucking little children God was knitting in my womb. We were falling in love with them, despite constant reminders that we might never hold them in our arms.

One morning in mid-April, the ultrasound technician said she could tell us the sex of our children if we wanted to know. We did.

"Baby B is a boy," she said, gesturing to the little creature with the button nose and penchant for rapid-fire kicks.

"And Baby A," she said, pointing to the one more interested in sleeping and hiccupping than performing for the ultrasound probe, "is a girl."

John and I cheered, thrilled to have one of each. Our elation evaporated a few minutes later, when the frowning technician gestured to what looked like an extra fold of skin on the back of one baby's neck, a sign of Down syndrome. I felt my palms go icy as she called in the perinatologist on duty that day, a woman with a better bedside manner than her male colleagues. The doctor acknowledged the unusual bump but cautioned against jumping to conclusions.

"Don't go borrowing trouble," she said, patting my growing belly. "Let's just focus on keeping these babies alive."

I knew her approach was right, since there was nothing John and I would do differently if our baby had Down syndrome. Still, it felt like a blow. One of our children might suffer a serious genetic disorder—if our children survived at all.

The new perinatologist took me off the aspirin immediately and put me on a stricter form of bed rest. No more walks, no more travel, no more anything for most of the day, she said, other than the occasional trek to the bathroom or kitchen. I was happy to comply, glad to finally find a physician who gave me permission to do what I had wanted to do all along: listen to my intuition and put my babies' health first. Yet even she made no promises about how much her advice would help. The bleed now surrounded the babies on nearly every side. It seemed only a matter of time before it burst through their placental sacs.

That afternoon John and I returned home, flopped onto our bed with our shoes still on, and held hands in the silence. I noticed a tear escaping down his cheek—the first I had seen since our bleeding ordeal began—and I felt my own hope fading. It seemed so unfair. Why would God bring us this close to parenthood, then yank it out of our grasp?

## Turning to Mary

Four years of infertility had introduced John and me to dozens of saints known for helping with difficult conceptions and pregnancies. We felt a special closeness to Saint Gianna Beretta Molla, an Italian physician, wife, and mother to whom Cardinal Raymond Burke had introduced us while he was archbishop of St. Louis, by giving us a relic of her clothing and confiding her reputation for helping infertile couples. We also sought heavenly help from Mother Teresa, whose successor, Sister Nirmala Joshi, once told us that babies were Mother's celestial specialty; Saint Gerard Majella, an Italian religious brother whose namesake parish near our home included a mini-shrine for aspiring and expectant mothers; and John Paul, a tireless advocate for the unborn who had not yet been beatified at that point but who struck us as a powerful intercessor all the same. Whenever we prayed for children, John and I would close our prayers with a litany to these special patrons. We always saved the best for last: Mary, mother of Jesus and Queen of Saints.

We had continued that habit after we learned of my pregnancy. It felt only natural to seek protection for our babies from the woman who had carried the baby Jesus in her womb, a woman whose maternal advocacy we believed had played a uniquely powerful role in our children's conception. When we realized those children might not survive to birth, it was Mary to whom we instinctively turned in our distress, pleading that our Blessed Mother once again intercede to her son for our cause.

Turning to Mary had not always been easy for John or me. As a Protestant, John grew up regarding Marian devotion as odd and unbiblical. He changed his mind in his twenties, as his study of scripture and church tradition and his own prayer experiences convinced him to embrace the Catholic faith and Mary's role in it. My esteem for Mary grew more gradually, after decades spent alternately ignoring her, fearing her intrusion, and fleeing to her for help.

Like many Catholics born after the Second Vatican Council, which closed in 1965, I grew up viewing Mary with some ambivalence. On the one hand, I knew that Catholic tradition always has encouraged great reverence for Mary and I felt a natural affection for her. On the other, I feared focusing on her too much lest I become one of those retrograde, "pre–Vatican II" Catholics who elevates Mary to a place that belongs to Jesus alone. It did not help that Mary's life had unfolded two millennia before mine, and that she had left behind no books or diaries to help me connect with her as I had with other, more modern women saints. I knew too little about Mary to feel genuinely close to her and felt too wary of Marian piety to learn more. So I had spent the first twenty years of my life regarding the exercise of Marian devotion the way a twelve-year-old boy thinks of kissing his mother good-bye: It's fine for toddlers or even older children, provided it's a special occasion and you're safe in the privacy of your own home, but showing such affection in public is risky and embarrassing.

I remember the first time I felt such embarrassment. I was six years old, playing T-ball in a city league in Tallahassee, Florida, where the majority of my first-grade teammates did not attend my Catholic school. As we jogged out to the field together between innings, a fellow infielder asked if I was Catholic.

"Yes," I said, feeling a surge of pride.

She scrunched up her freckled nose as if sucking a lemon.

"You Catholics worship Mary," she said.

"No, we don't."

"Yes, you do. You have all those statues of her."

"But we don't worship her."

"Yes, you do," she called over her shoulder, as she darted left to take her place at third base. "My daddy said so."

That night I asked my father about it. He said I was right; we didn't worship Mary. But we did ask Mary to ask Jesus to help us, because she is Jesus's mother and he pays special attention to her. Although his answer made sense to me, I never forgot the shame I felt at my first apologetics debate—and the danger that lurks in defending Mary too publicly.

I felt that embarrassment again years later, while traveling in Europe with a practicing Catholic friend shortly after college. We popped into a historic cathedral for a visit, and I pulled out a pamphlet on Mary that I had picked up somewhere along the way. As I cracked it open, my friend asked why I was bothering with Mary when I could focus solely on Jesus. I fell mute, not knowing how to answer.

I posed a similar question to a Dominican priest friend not long afterward, as he was describing his deepening personal devotion to Mary. It was not that I doubted Mary's power as an intercessor, I told him; hastily offered prayers for her help had delivered me from too many scrapes to question her pull with her divine son. It was just that Mary's place in my faith remained limited largely to disaster relief. I saw her as a sort of secret spiritual weapon, a heavenly Wonder Woman who could get you out of just about any jam even if you had ignored her since your last fix. I struggled to see what Mary could teach me beyond the obvious:

that I should turn to God, and his friends in heaven, when I needed help.

My curiosity about Mary began to grow as I learned more about Catholic teaching on Mary both before and after Vatican II. I discovered that Mary's designation as "Mother of God" was not a recent Catholic quirk but a truth affirmed at the fifth-century Council of Ephesus, in response to the Nestorian heresy that held that Mary was only mother of the human Jesus. The church had rejected that diluted view of Mary as an attack on the divinity of Christ.

I also learned that the Second Vatican Council fathers never intended to shoo Mary to the margins of Catholic life. The discomfort and even disdain for Marian devotion that I sensed in some of my Catholic parishes and schools growing up were based not on authentic council teaching but on an ill-defined "spirit of Vatican II" that erred in giving Mary and her fellow saints short shrift. In reality, the council fathers had pointedly praised Mary in their landmark 1964 document, "Light of the Nations," as "exalted above all angels and men to a place second only to her son" and said devotion to Mary must be "generously fostered" and "highly esteemed."

Yet the council fathers noted in that same document that excesses of Marian devotion could distract from Christ and confuse non-Catholics. I knew they were right. My suspicion of Marian piety had been stoked by encounters with Catholics who succumbed to such excesses: the apparition junkies who uncritically embraced rumors of each new Marian sighting, even after the church declared such sightings hoaxes; the well-intentioned but inattentive churchgoers who spent entire Masses praying their rosaries while ignoring the liturgical prayers of the priest and congregation; the monomaniacal novena peddlers who cornered me in church pews and insisted that if I prayed this particular prayer to Mary under this particular title for this particular number of days, there was no way God could *not* grant my petition, whatever it was.

In "Light of the Nations," the council fathers caution against such "false exaggeration" of Marian piety, noting that devotion to Mary must be distinguished from the adoration due to God alone. True devotion to Mary must always lead closer to Christ and remain rooted in Christ, they write, "the source of all truth, sanctity, and devotion." Such authentic Marian devotion "consists neither in sterile or transitory affection, nor in a certain vain credulity, but proceeds from true faith, by which we are led to recognize the excellence of the Mother of God, and we are moved to a filial love towards our mother and to the imitation of her virtues."

The progression that the council fathers described—from a sentimental, almost magical view of Mary to genuine affection, admiration, and a desire to imitate her virtues—slowly unfolded in my life as I learned more about Mary's role in salvation history. The Marian devotion that would anchor me amid the storms of my high-risk pregnancy at age thirty-four was the fruit of a few simple questions I first began asking in my early twenties: Who, exactly, is this mysterious woman of God? Why should I cultivate a relationship with her? And how can devotion to Mary make me a better follower of Christ?

## Biblical Heroine

At first glance, scripture seems curiously quiet about Mary. Her New Testament appearances are rare and her quotes even rarer. Although the Acts of the Apostles and all four Gospels mention Mary by name, the story of the Annunciation—in which the angel announces to this young virgin that she will miraculously conceive the Son of God in her womb—appears only in Luke's Gospel. Even there, we find few words attributed to Mary: a brief exchange with the angel Gabriel, a song of praise uttered while visiting her cousin Elizabeth, and a two-sentence query to the child Jesus after she finds him preaching in Jerusalem's temple. In John's Gospel, Mary speaks briefly at the wedding at Cana but takes a subdued tone. After she tells Jesus that the newlyweds have no wine and he replies that "my hour has not yet come," Mary discreetly advises the servants to "do whatever he tells you" (John 2:5). Jesus then performs his first public miracle: He instructs the servants to fill the jugs with water, which he transforms into wine. The wine steward raves about the quality of Jesus's creation. Mary, meanwhile, recedes into the background, with nothing more to say.

In a mass-media culture that equates influence with verbosity and visibility, it's tempting to look at Mary's low profile in scripture and conclude that she is little more than a bit player in the divine drama. Many Christians have done just that, dismissing Marian devotion in general—and Catholic Marian dogmas defined in recent centuries in particular—as suspiciously unbiblical add-ons with no place in serious Christianity.

From a strictly proof-texting point of view, their suspicion makes sense. The relative scarcity of scripture verses referring directly to Mary can make Catholic teachings about her tough to swallow, if one starts from the assumption that anything not spelled out explicitly in scripture cannot count as part of the deposit of faith. Of course, many biblical purists who begin with this assumption have no qualms about reciting creeds crafted centuries after Jesus walked the earth or revering a Bible that was, itself, compiled by the church.

Catholics take a different view: that both scripture and tradition lead us to truth with the magisterium, or teaching authority of the church, guiding our understanding of each. The Bible does not interpret itself, in other words; it must be interpreted by the church that assembled it. In this view, the church's two-thousand-year history of Marian devotion informs the way we read scripture references to Mary, and the church's teaching authority helps us grasp new biblical insights about her even now. As Catholic convert David Mills explains in his book *Discovering Mary*, "The Church has, or indeed is, a living tradition, and . . . imposes no time limit on what God may teach her."

Reading scripture through this lens reveals references to Mary in the Old Testament as well as the New. Her role in God's plan is foreshadowed as early as the Bible's first book, when God tells the serpent: "I will put enmity between you and the woman, and between your offspring and hers; he will strike your head, and you will strike his heel" (Gen. 3:15). The church traditionally has regarded Mary as the "New Eve" spoken of here, the obedient woman whose divine son, the "New Adam," will crush Satan's head and reverse the curse incurred by the disobedience of the first Adam and Eve. Another allusion to Mary appears in the book of Isaiah, which predicts that "a virgin shall conceive, and bear a son, and shall call his name Immanuel" (Isa. 7:14).

Beyond such specific references, a pattern emerges throughout the Hebrew scriptures in which women play significant, even heroic roles in advancing salvation history. Think Sarah, Rachel, Hannah, Esther, and Judith. As Pope Benedict XVI notes in *Daughter Zion,* a book he wrote before his election to the papacy, many of these women were mothers once scorned for their barrenness but ultimately blessed for their faith. Their "barren-but-blessed" status in Judaism stands in stark contrast to the status of such women in pagan religions, where fertility cults celebrated promiscuity and infertility signified worthlessness. Benedict cites this reversal of earthly expectations as an Old Testament precursor to Mary's virginal conception of Jesus and to her virginity itself, which the Catholic Church holds that she preserved throughout her lifetime. Mary's self-emptying act of saying "yes" to God at the Annunciation—and her acceptance of all the suffering and social peril that "yes" would entail for a young woman in her situation—was the culmination of a long biblical tradition of faithful women finding fulfillment by surrendering to God's surprising will: "In this 'new birth' . . . which simultaneously included the abandonment of earthly fertility, of self-disposal, and of the autonomous planning of one's own life, Mary as Mother is truly 'the bearer of God'; she is more than the organ of a fortuitous corporeal event. To bear the 'son' includes the surrender of oneself into barrenness. Now it becomes clear why barrenness is the condition of fruitfulness—the mystery of the Old Testament mothers becomes transparent in Mary. It receives its meaning in Christian virginity beginning with Mary."

The very concept of Christian virginity—that some women and men are called to consecrate themselves totally to God, body and soul—is profoundly countercultural in a society that treats sexual self-restraint as evidence of neurosis. And the Catholic teaching that Mary not only conceived Jesus as a virgin but remained a virgin after his birth, even through her marriage to Joseph, strikes many modern observers as an arcane, unnecessary doctrine, evidence of Catholicism's aversion to women's sexuality.

As Benedict's argument about barren-but-blessed biblical heroines suggests, though, the virgin birth and perpetual virginity of Mary represent not the triumph of chauvinism but blows against it. In a world always tempted to prize women more for their fecundity and sexual allure than for their souls—a temptation typified by the ancient "goddess" cults in which prostitution, forced abortions, and female infanticide were commonplace—Mary's perpetual virginity challenges the status quo. Her complete consecration to God confirms the value and importance of women for their own sakes, even apart from their ability to provide sexual pleasure or large numbers of heirs to men. As Edith Stein puts it, the ideal of Christian virginity embodied in Mary presents a "basic change in the status of woman" affecting all women, whether single, consecrated, or married. Marriage and motherhood are no longer the only ways a woman can serve God, Edith says, and even for those who choose marriage and motherhood, Mary's total gift of self to God amid motherhood reminds them that their first priority is fidelity to God.

## Mary in the Gospels

Mary's fidelity to God finds its clearest biblical manifestation in the stories of the Annunciation and the Visitation, both found in the first chapter of Luke. The Annunciation opens with the angel

Gabriel's greeting to Mary: "Hail, full of grace! The Lord is with you." Gabriel tells the perplexed young virgin that she has "found favor with God" and will conceive his son in her womb. Mary asks the obvious question—"How can this be, since I have no relations with a man?"—and Gabriel answers that this conception will be an act of God, just as was the late-in-life pregnancy of her once-barren cousin, Elizabeth. Mary's answer is simple and profound: "Behold, I am the handmaid of the Lord. Let it be done unto me according to your word" (Luke 1:26–38).

Mary then travels to the hill country for the Visitation to Elizabeth. As soon as the pregnant cousins see each other, Elizabeth's unborn child, John the Baptist, leaps in his mother's womb. Elizabeth greets Mary in words similar to those of Gabriel, hailing her as "blessed among women" and "the mother of my Lord." Elizabeth praises Mary not only for the divine child she bears in her womb but for the faith that allowed Mary to first welcome that child in her heart: "Blessed is she who believed that there would be a fulfillment of what was spoken to her by the Lord" (Luke 1:45). Mary answers with her Magnificat, a hymn of humble gratitude for the graces God has given her:

*My soul proclaims the greatness of the Lord,*
*my spirit rejoices in God my savior*
*for he has looked with favor on his lowly servant.*

*From this day all generations will call me blessed;*
*the Almighty has done great things for me,*
*and holy is his name.*

*Luke 1:46–49*

The church always has seen great significance in the details of these two stories. For starters, there is Gabriel's greeting to Mary ("full of grace"), which the church reads as a reference to a unique privilege that God bestowed on Mary: complete freedom from both original and personal sin from the moment of her conception. Known as the Immaculate Conception, this singular gift from God allowed Mary to become the "New Eve," a woman filled entirely with his grace throughout her life. It liberated her to give God her complete "yes" at the Annunciation, a "yes" purified of any traces of doubt, selfishness, or vainglory.

Mary's preservation from the curse of original sin did not erase her humanity or her need for redemption. She simply received that redemption, as the Second Vatican Council fathers put it, "in a more exalted fashion, by reason of the merits of her son." This special gift prepared Mary for her special mission as the Mother of God. As Bishop Fulton Sheen explains in *The World's First Love*:

> There *had* to be some such creature as Mary—otherwise God would have found no one in whom He could fittingly have taken His human origin. An honest politician seeking civic reforms looks about for honest assistants. The Son of God beginning a new creation searched for some of that Goodness which existed before sin took over. There would have been, in some minds, a doubt about the Power of God if He had not shown a special favor to the woman who was to be His Mother. Certainly what God gave to Eve, He would not refuse to His own Mother.

Related to Mary's unique freedom from sin is the Catholic doctrine of her Assumption, which holds that Mary's body did not suffer decay when her earthly life ended and that she is already united to God, body and soul, in heaven. She has experienced, in other words, the full redemption and resurrection of the body that the rest of us await at the final judgment. This teaching stems from a venerable tradition in both East and West, where believers for millennia have considered it only logical that the God who preserved Mary from sin and corruption throughout her life, and who made his dwelling in her body, would continue to preserve her body from corruption after her life on earth ended. As Benedict, then Cardinal Joseph Ratzinger, notes in *Daughter Zion,* Mary's Assumption is inextricably entwined with her Immaculate Conception, with that perfect purity of heart that allowed God's grace to fill every inch of her soul, leaving no room for sin or its corrupting consequences. "Where the totality of grace is, there is the totality of salvation," writes Benedict, who describes the dogma of Mary's Assumption as "the highest degree of canonization" for the woman who predicted that "all generations will call me blessed."

Generations have called Mary blessed not only because of her unique privileges, but because of the role she plays in guiding the rest of us toward union with God—the complete, body-soul union she already enjoys. This guiding role is one played by all of the saints, but Mary's guidance takes on a distinctly maternal character. Two stories in John's Gospel provide snapshots of Mary in this maternal role. The first is the wedding at Cana, which shows her advocating on behalf of the newlyweds who run short of wine—a mundane matter that proves no problem is too small to warrant Mary's maternal intercession. The second is the story of Jesus's final words to John from the cross, where he instructs John to adopt Mary as his own mother:

> When Jesus saw his mother and the disciple whom he loved standing beside her, he said to his mother, "Woman, behold your son." Then he said to the disciple, "Behold your mother." And from that hour the disciple took her into his home.
>
> *John 19:26–27*

In his 1987 encyclical *Mother of the Redeemer,* John Paul argues that this passage reveals Jesus's desire to give Mary "as mother to every single individual and all mankind." John's response to this gift—he "took her into his home"—shows how we should respond, too: by welcoming Mary into our homes and hearts, entrusting to her maternal care our spiritual growth and daily concerns.

John Paul cautions that we must never separate Mary's maternal role from Jesus, whom the church, following Saint Paul in scripture, identifies as the "one mediator" between God and humanity. As the Second Vatican Council fathers put it, Mary's spiritual motherhood "in no way obscures or diminishes this unique mediation of Christ, but rather shows its power. . . . [Mary's influence] flows forth from the superabundance of the merits of Christ, rests on his mediation, depends entirely on it and draws all its power from it. It does not hinder in any way the immediate union of the faithful with Christ but on the contrary fosters it." In other words, we should turn to Mary as a helper on our path to union with Christ because he told us to do so, never forgetting that all power originates in God alone.

## Model and Mother

With all her unique privileges, Mary sometimes can seem too remote to understand our messy lives. How can you relate to someone who never violated God's will even in the slightest matter and already lives in body-soul bliss with God? How, as a woman, can you avoid feeling a twinge of envy toward this most "blessed among women" who embodies all the feminine holiness and virtues you lack? Sure, Mary navigated life in our fallen world. Yet she did so free from the inborn tendency to sin. How hard could her life have been, really?

In my struggles with these questions, I found it surprising and somewhat reassuring to discover how many theologians believe Mary had it tougher than the rest of us, because her sinless nature made living in our sinful world especially painful. Like Jesus, Mary probably approached the world with acute sensitivity, alert to both the tiniest whispers of God's voice and the slightest suffering in the lives of others. The casual cruelties and everyday injustices we inflict without thinking probably disturbed Mary more than they would someone with a calloused, sin-hardened soul. And the torture and Crucifixion of her innocent son must have ripped her heart in two. Luke alludes to Mary's sorrow in his story of Jesus's presentation at the temple, where the prophet Simeon holds the infant Jesus aloft and warns Mary that her son is destined "to be a sign that will be opposed . . . and a sword will pierce your own heart too" (Luke 2:34–35).

Luke does not say how Mary reacted to Simeon's prophecy. Yet two other stories in the same chapter give us a clue. When shepherds she did not know came to adore her newborn baby and informed her that an angel had told them her son would save the world, Mary responded not by gloating or grilling them. Instead, Luke says, "Mary treasured all these words and pondered them in her heart" (Luke 2:19). She did the same upon finding her twelve-year-old son preaching in Jerusalem's temple, after a three-day search that left her and Joseph panicked. Mary asks Jesus why he gave them such a scare. He answers with a question: "Did you not know that I must be in my father's house?" Mary "did not understand what he said to them," Luke says, but she "treasured all these things in her heart" (Luke 2:49–51).

Of all of her gifts, Mary's contemplative approach to life—her habit of prayerfully pondering life's joys and sorrows in her heart—surprised and challenged me the most. Like most women raised in the wake of the modern feminist movement, I grew up equating feminine strength with outspokenness and action. I knew that godly women often are called to stand up and speak out. Mary reminded me of another truth: that a woman's greatest strength comes from silent communion with God, and sometimes the most radical thing she can do is not rant and rave but watch and pray.

Such revelations made me wonder how I ever dismissed Mary as a one-dimensional saint about whom there was nothing much to know and from whom there was nothing much to learn. Through my studies of her life and spirituality, Mary was beginning to feel real to me, more real than any saint ever had. And though her holiness sometimes intimidated me, I found myself increasingly attracted to her—not simply as a model but as a mother.

Mary's motherhood took on new meaning for me one afternoon in my mid-twenties, when I stopped in the church where I was baptized in Green Bay, Wisconsin. My mom and I were there together, taking a break from visiting my aged grandmother. The trip had been a little rough, filled with the usual tensions that surface when three generations of women gather under one roof. I remember marveling as I sat in a pew near the altar how much closer my mother and I were than she was to her mother, yet even our relationship had its share of sticky, unresolved issues. I thought of how my relationship with my own children would be: probably loving and close but still marked by some discord and disappointment, most of it stemming from mistakes I would make as a mother. How wonderful it would be if I could be a perfect mother, a completely flawless, selfless nurturer whose loving guidance never erred. *Not going to happen,* I thought glumly as I glanced around the sanctuary and imagined my grandmother aspiring to the same goal in the same church decades earlier. There is no such thing as a perfect mother.

Just then, my eyes landed on a statue of Mary near the altar. As arresting as the royal blue of her robes was the message I heard interiorly: *This is your mother; this is the perfect mother you long to have and to be.* I realized that Mary was as real a mother to me as the one who bore me in her womb, and that she loved me with the same fierce, fathomless love that any good mother feels for her child—a love all the more powerful because it stems from her uniquely pure maternal heart.

I looked over to Mom, her eyes closed in prayer before the same altar and same statue, and realized: Mary is her mother, too. Mary's motherhood is universal. It encompasses everyone yet seeks to possess no one. Rather than driving a wedge between earthly mothers and their children or making ordinary mothers feel inadequate, Mary's maternal love allows us to respond with gentleness to our own failings and those of our loved ones, because we know that our heavenly mother can help fill in the gaps of our imperfect human relationships. She even can help fill in the gaps of our relationship with her son, by interceding for us to receive the grace to follow him more closely in every part of life, including family life.

That insight catapulted me to a new level in my devotion to the Mother of God. My habit of turning to Mary with my concerns intensified, and the more I turned to Mary, the more I felt drawn to loving, serving, and imitating her son. When I would pray to Mary for a favor, it was invariably Jesus I thanked when I received it. I found myself listening more closely to the promptings of the Holy Spirit and asking myself in tricky situations: What would Mary do? The question most often arose when I faced some slight or insult that normally would provoke me to an angry outburst or a sullen bout of self-pity. I still felt those temptations and often succumbed to them. Yet looking to Mary—a woman who shared my status as a creature but not my sinfulness—helped me imagine a different response. When I remembered to make them, my quick, furtive pleas for her help gave me just the jolt of strength I needed to overcome temptation and opt for gentleness instead.

My appreciation for Mary continued to grow after I met John. Seeing this born-and-bred Protestant initially wrestle with and then ardently embrace Mary's role as his spiritual mother edified and humbled me. Marian devotion quickly became a key feature of our shared spiritual life. We started saying the Hail Holy Queen, a traditional Marian prayer, together by phone each night before bed. That habit continued after our engagement and my move to Washington, DC, where I began praying a silent Hail Mary each day at noon—a quick way to remember Jesus and

Mary in the middle of the workday. By the time our wedding day arrived, John and I felt strongly that we should honor the Mother of God with flowers, hymns, and a special prayer at our nuptial Mass. We knelt before an icon of Our Lady of Perpetual Help that unusually warm December day, scooted as close together as the folds of my white satin dress would allow, and prayed that Mary would keep us united to Jesus and each other through married life's fiercest trials.

When the first of those trials arrived in the form of our infertility diagnosis, our Marian devotion deepened again. I began reaching out to Mary on a daily, often hourly, basis while enduring invasive exams and mourning the arrival of my monthly periods, experiences I knew another woman could understand. John and I started visiting Marian shrines near our home to implore her help in conceiving, and we took several international pilgrimages to church-approved apparition sites. In 2005 we walked on our knees across the massive plaza at the Shrine of Our Lady of Guadalupe in Mexico City, following a traditional penitential practice that left me with holes in my jeans and a sure sense that the beautiful woman pictured on that five-hundred-year-old *tilma* would help us become parents. In 2006 we hiked the hot, dusty Way of the Cross at Fatima in Portugal and prayed for a child in the same spot where three shepherd children saw Mary in 1917.

Our most memorable Marian pilgrimage came in May 2006, when we crossed the French Pyrenees into the little village of Lourdes. A mountain spring and rough-hewn grotto there has been associated with medical miracles ever since a poor girl named Bernadette saw visions of Mary at that spot in 1858. The nightly candlelit rosary processions were a highlight of the trip, as John and I strolled through the picturesque Lourdes complex with thousands of people of every language and race, all united in prayer and led by the wheelchair-bound pilgrims who receive pride of place in any Lourdes celebration. We wanted the full Lourdes experience, so we separated into the men's and women's lines at the famous Lourdes baths, stripped to nothing but a towel and allowed efficient strangers in private bathing rooms to dunk us in the ice-cold water as we murmured a Hail Mary for our intentions. I was not sure the bath healed me of anything, but like my scabbed-knee trek across the Guadalupe shrine, it surely shaved off a few layers of pride.

I felt particularly buoyed by an experience I had while milling about the back of the old Lourdes church on the last day of our visit. I was surrounded by people speaking in every language but my own. Suddenly, I overheard Luke's Gospel being read in English, coming from behind a little side door I barely had noticed when I entered the sanctuary. The snippet I heard was from the Annunciation, where Gabriel tells Mary of Elizabeth's miraculous pregnancy: "And now, your relative Elizabeth in her old age has also conceived a son; and this is the sixth month for her who was said to be barren. For nothing will be impossible for God" (Luke 1:36–37). Those words —"nothing will be impossible for God"— rang in my ears, and I felt sure that Mary had meant for me to hear them.

I returned home to face three more years of infertility before my prayers for pregnancy were answered. Yet I never forgot that experience or the strong sense I received on each of our pilgrimages that Mary intended to help John and me become parents. Nor did I fail to notice that two weeks after we started reciting our nightly rosary together, we were blessed with the pregnancy that had eluded us for years.

Those memories took on particular significance as I faced the possible loss of our unborn children in April 2009, a decade after I had first begun my quest to get to know Mary. I wanted desperately to believe that the God who made all things possible would not rescind his miracle so soon after delivering it. And I prayed more fervently than ever for Mary's intercession, hoping that the Blessed Mother who had brought us this far would not forsake us now.

## Waiting with Mary

As my second trimester swung into full gear and my belly began to expand, John and I stormed heaven for our babies. We started spreading news of the pregnancy to relatives and friends and requesting their prayers, specifically to Mary under the title of Our Lady of Lourdes. I had plenty of time for prayer, spiritual reading, and chats with friends, since I spent most of my waking hours lying on our living room couch, following my bed-rest regimen.

My next doctor's appointment, at the end of April, brought mixed news. The babies were still growing, and the extra fold of skin spotted on my previous ultrasound turned out to be a shadow, not a sign of Down syndrome. My bleeding was worse, though; the external flow of bright red blood was almost continuous now. And the odd quivers I was feeling in my abdomen were not baby kicks but contractions—a sign that I might be headed for preterm labor, something for which I already faced heightened risk as a mother of twins. I was only seventeen weeks into my pregnancy; term for twins was thirty-six. If my babies debuted before thirty-two weeks, they likely would face serious complications.

If they arrived before twenty-four weeks, the doctors said, they would die.

The hardest part about receiving such news was what I had to do afterward: go home and lie alone on my couch, unable to do anything more for my babies than pray. As the hours and days dragged on, I began to think a lot about waiting—the waiting I had done in my own life, usually grudgingly, and the waiting Mary did in the nine months that she carried Jesus. It could not have been an easy pregnancy. Here she was, a peasant girl probably no older than fifteen, suddenly facing motherhood and the possible collapse of her nascent marriage to a man who initially greeted her surprise pregnancy with plans to divorce her. She spent her first trimester away from home, tending to a pregnant cousin. She spent the end of her third trimester trudging with Joseph through the desert. She delivered her baby in a barn—not exactly an optimal birth plan—then spent her postpartum recovery entertaining a parade of strangers in her not-so-plush maternity suite. When she finally bid farewell to her last uninvited guest, her husband awakened her in the middle of the night and told her they needed to flee to Egypt because powerful people wanted her baby dead.

Motherhood only got harder for Mary as the years went on. Simeon's prophecy surely rang in her ears as she endured the exile in Egypt, lost the child Jesus in Jerusalem, met her bloodied son face-to-face during his trek to Calvary, and finally felt the crushing weight of his battered, lifeless body in her arms. Mary may have been the perfect mother, but very little about her earthly experience of motherhood was perfect.

That thought consoled me as I struggled to make sense of my own rocky road to motherhood. I felt so helpless sprawled there on that couch, and I imagined Mary knew the feeling. I thought of her standing under her son's cross. What strength she had to remain there in the face of so much suffering, refusing to succumb to bitterness or self-pity or the temptation to flee as nearly all his apostles had. Mary may not have understood what was happening to her son; Jesus's death probably felt to her like a world-ending blow. Yet she stayed and prayed anyway, trusting that God would bring good out of this apparent disaster. Her willingness to set aside her own dreams for her child and embrace God's mysterious will instead made Mary a cooperator in, rather than an obstacle to, Christ's saving mission. As Saint Catherine of Siena writes, "[Jesus] ran like one in love, enduring pain, disgrace, and abuse, all the way to his shameful death on the cross. Mary did exactly the same . . . for she could desire nothing but God's honor and the salvation of his creatures. This is why the Doctors [of the Church] tell us, referring to Mary's immense love, that she would have made a ladder of her very self to put her son on the cross if there had been no other way. All this was because her son's will remained within her."

Mary's sacrificial, liberating love offers a bracing counterpoint to the white-knuckled perfectionism that masquerades as maternal competence in our culture today. Given my natural tendency toward perfectionism, it occurred to me that perhaps God was using my tumultuous pregnancy and Mary's example to teach me the virtue I would need most as a mother: a willingness to surrender. I had no guarantee that my babies would survive to birth. But if they did, and my dreams of motherhood came true, I knew I would need to resist again and again the tug toward maternal perfectionism—toward the furious insistence that my life and the lives of my children unfold the way I think best. If anyone could help me win that battle, it was Mary, the sorrowful mother whose bumpy maternal ride ended in eternal glory.

## No Explanation

On a Thursday afternoon in mid-May, the month traditionally associated with Mary, John and I headed to the hospital for another ultrasound. We were too nervous to speak as he pushed my wheelchair from the lobby to the perinatal center. I tried to avert my eyes from the parade of beaming new mothers whose wheelchairs passed mine, women cradling the sort of plump, healthy newborns I might never take home. I was not quite five months pregnant and not quite sure if that day's sonogram would find my babies alive or dead.

We breathed a sigh of relief when the ultrasound confirmed our babies' heartbeats and showed their little bodies squirming across the screen. Minutes later, my perinatologist bounded into the room waving our ultrasound images.

"Your babies are growing," she said. "And the bleed has not spread."

It was the first good news we had heard about the bleed since it began, and we were sure it was the fruit of prayer. When the doctor left the room, John and I squeezed hands and whispered a Hail Mary in thanksgiving.

At our next checkup two weeks later, the bleed looked even smaller. Within a month, it had vanished.

"What happened?" I asked the doctor.

"It's a miracle," she answered.

I did not know what to make of her comment, since she did not strike me as the religious type. When I pressed her for details at the next visit, she said she and her colleagues had puzzled over my case and could not make sense of the rapid healing. One of them even had requested photos of my twins when they were born so he could include them in the case file he was preparing for his medical students. He wanted them to study my pregnancy, she said, "because it was the worst bleed he had ever seen, and it was followed by an unexplained resolution."

For our part, John and I needed no explanation. Jesus had just sent us another miracle.

## Labor Pains

As spring melted into summer, my doctor took me off bed rest and I reveled in my newfound liberation. John and I started preparing the nursery and reading up on newborn sleep habits. I waddled back into daily Mass for the first time in months. My friends began planning a shower. Life was good.

My freewheeling days did not last long. Shortly after I got off bed rest for bleeding, I was put on again for preterm labor, after a scare at thirty-one weeks sent me to the hospital. The doctors were worried about the increasingly severe contractions I experienced whenever I took walks outside or spent the day on my feet. I still managed to enjoy a beautiful baby shower on the feast of Mary's Assumption and to take the occasional outing after that. But I resumed spending most of my time on the couch, praying to make it to the thirty-six-week mark. Mary once again became my constant companion, the prayerful, waiting mother to whom I entrusted my little ones.

On September 13, a balmy Sunday that marked my thirty-sixth week of pregnancy, John and I visited sprawling Forest Park in the heart of St. Louis before attending evening Mass at the Cathedral Basilica. The doctors had said I was free to do as I pleased at that point, so I had joined John for a three-hour stroll through the park. John filmed video of me and my basketball-sized belly as I told the camera how excited we were to meet our babies. The walk wore me out, and by the time I edged myself into bed at eight that night, I was exhausted. Pain kept me awake, however, and I soon realized I was in labor.

Like just about everything else in my life, I had opinions about what sort of birth experience I wanted. I planned to be aware and involved, lucid enough to hold and nurse my babies as soon as they were born, and given ample opportunities to bond with them in their first few days of life. I wanted no forceps or suction used on them, no episiotomy on me, and no C-section if I could avoid it. I had no illusions about my pain tolerance—I knew natural childbirth was not for me—but I intended to delay receiving the epidural as long as possible, in hopes of making labor progress more quickly. I also wanted to avoid the drugs my friends had warned me about: Pitocin, which speeds up labor but also can make it more painful and risky, and magnesium sulfate, an anti-seizure medication with psychedelic, nauseating side effects that prevent a mother from breast-feeding or caring for a newborn for the first twenty-four hours after receiving it.

Reality made quick work of my fantasy birth plan. I spent nearly twenty-two hours in labor, complete with the Pitocin I did not want and the use of forceps, suction, and an episiotomy to coax out my daughter, who fought valiantly to stay in my womb. When she finally emerged at 5:26 P.M. that Monday, the nurses swept her away before I could see her face. They busied themselves taking her footprints and ordering John to pose for pictures with her, while I called out weakly from the operating table, begging someone to let me glimpse my baby girl.

The doctors, meanwhile, had turned their focus to my baby boy. When my obstetrician reached inside me to deliver him, he discovered that the baby had flipped positions and his umbilical cord was poised to exit the womb before him. If that happened, his body would put pressure on the cord and cut off his blood supply, suffocating him. The doctor began frantically tossing me around the table like a slab of beef, barking orders at his assistants as they struggled to get my son into position.

"We need to do an emergency C-section," he finally shouted as swarms of physicians and nurses scurried to scrub for surgery.

The epidural had left me shivering uncontrollably at that point, and I could not keep still. An anesthesiologist held my left arm down as a nurse pinned my right. I strained for a glimpse of John, still sequestered with the nurses and the daughter I had not seen. His eyes met mine and were as wide as saucers. I knew our son was in trouble.

I blinked back tears as I stared at the fluorescent lights above me and began stuttering aloud the Hail Marys that I had been saying silently to myself all afternoon. I felt too weak to say the whole prayer, so I just repeated the first two lines over and over again: "Hail Mary, full of grace, / The Lord is with thee . . ."

Lying cruciform on the operating table with the doctor frantically cutting my baby out of my womb, I realized what day it was: September 14, feast of the Triumph of the Cross. I felt a flash of dark humor as I remembered how often I had begged Jesus to let me have the full experience of biological motherhood: baby bump, labor pains, and all. Now he was answering my prayer. He was giving me everything, all right. I hoped that this feast day was a good sign, that if I could just hold on a little longer, my suffering, like his, would end in triumph.

My son was born twenty minutes after my daughter, looking blue but pinking up quickly with the help of an oxygen mask. The nurses finally consented to let me hold my two squawking bundles soon afterward. I cried when I saw them, more from exhaustion than from joy, and they were yanked away a moment later. I spent the next few days fighting for opportunities to see them amid complications from my own recovery, including a second sleepless night with the magnesium sulfate treatment for preeclampsia that I had hoped to avoid, my son's brief stint in the neonatal intensive care unit, and the resistance of some hospital staffers who scoffed at my plan to breast-feed twins.

It was not until John and I returned from the hospital four days after the birth that I finally felt free to revel in the amazing gifts God had given us. As we stood in our living room, staring at two perfectly formed, nearly six-pound babies snoozing in matching pink and blue car seats, we exchanged a teary embrace. The birth, like the pregnancy and years of waiting that preceded it, had been rough. Nothing about my journey to motherhood had proceeded as planned. But we were home now. This was our family, finally, and we were home.

## A Litany of Thanks

We named our son John Patrick: John for his father and Patrick for my father, Thomas Patrick. We resolved that he would be called by both names to avoid confusion between the two Johns in our home and to keep Dad's memory alive.

Our daughter's name had been chosen years earlier, when we first began asking our Blessed Mother to send us a rose from heaven. She was Maryrose Therese: Mary for the Mother of God, a name that also honored my mother, Mary; Rose because she was our little flower from heaven, and because I always had loved the name of my first patron saint, Rose of Lima; and Therese for the Little Flower and all the other Teresas we admired, including Teresa of Ávila, Mother Teresa, and Teresa Benedicta of the Cross, also known as Edith Stein.

Our children were baptized on November 1, the feast of All Saints. A young Jesuit priest friend of ours, Father Phil, performed the private ceremony in the glow of rainbow-colored rays streaming through our parish's stained-glass windows. A small group of family and friends attended. As I cradled an angelic, white-bonneted Maryrose in my arms and John held a wide-eyed John Patrick against his chest, we listened to Father Phil repeat the last stanza of the psalm we had chosen for the occasion:

*I believe that I shall see the goodness of the Lord in the land of the living.*
*Wait for the Lord, be stouthearted and wait for the Lord.*

*Psalm 27:13–14*

"John and Colleen waited for the Lord," he said in his homily, "and they have seen his goodness."

We prayed during the baptismal rite for our deceased loved ones, especially Dad. We also included a litany to the saints, sung a cappella by the priest, with all of us joining in the refrain. The litany opened by asking for mercy from each member of the Trinity: Father, Son, and Holy Spirit. Then we asked God's saints to intercede for us, that we, too, might someday join their ranks. We began with Mary, Queen of Saints, under the titles that meant the most to us:

*Holy Mary, Mother of God, pray for us.*
*Our Lady of Lourdes, pray for us.*
*Our Lady of Guadalupe, pray for us.*
*Our Lady of Fatima, pray for us.*

We included those who had helped us through our infertility trial:

*Saint Gianna, pray for us.*
*Saint Gerard, pray for us.*
*Servant of God Pope John Paul II, pray for us.*

And we made special mention of those women saints who had become some of my dearest friends:

*Saint Teresa of Ávila, pray for us.*
*Saint Thérèse of Lisieux, pray for us.*
*Saint Faustina, pray for us.*

*Saint Edith Stein, pray for us.*

*Blessed Mother Teresa, pray for us.*

As their names rang out, I thought back to all that had happened since that hot October morning fifteen years earlier when I had perched on my Milwaukee windowsill and wondered how to fill the emptiness inside me. I had seen so much, changed so much, hurt so much, and learned so much. I knew I still had much to learn—my journey as a wife was in its early stages, and my journey as a mother had just begun—but I marveled that God had transformed my life and priorities so radically since that day. And he had done it in a way that spiritually starved college student I once was never would have imagined: by introducing me to six women saints who taught me the true meaning of liberation.

Looking at the baptismal font where my babies soon would be blessed with holy water and welcomed into the Body of Christ, I thought of the Gospel story of the Samaritan woman at the well. She had trudged out of her house that hot, dusty day with no notion that she would meet God face-to-face. She intended only to execute a mundane chore, to get the bucket of water she needed to continue living the familiar but shallow life that seemed to be the best she could do. Jesus was waiting for her, though, waiting for the slightest opening to challenge her subsistence mind-set and introduce her to a supernatural joy and freedom she could hardly fathom.

"Everyone who drinks of this water will be thirsty again," Jesus told her, "but those who drink of the water that I will give them will never be thirsty. The water that I will give will become in them a spring of water gushing up to eternal life" (John 4:13–14).

On this day, standing beside my husband and holding the miracle babies I had thought I would never see, I felt like that Samaritan woman must have felt when she dropped her water jar and went running into the city, eager to tell the world about the man who showed her the truth about herself. Jesus, through his saints, had done the same for me. He had shown me the truth about myself, about my feminine nature and gifts and the way I could find lasting fulfillment as a woman. He had given me the living water that alone could quench the thirst I first identified on that windowsill when I was twenty. That living water was himself: his grace, his love, his peace. Although I knew I had many miles left to travel before I reached my destination, I felt overwhelmed by the blessings Jesus had lavished on me thus far. Among the greatest was what he and his friends in heaven had taught me in tough times: that God's love would be with me no matter what storms blew my way. And that love—if I continued to cling to it—would lead me safely to my eternal home.

As our litany of saints finally came to a close, we ended our song with this request:

*All you holy men and women, pray for us.*

And I knew, sure as the golden beams now bathing our little family in sunlight, that they would.

#  Acknowledgments 

This book would not exist if not for the ardent, insistent, and persistent encouragement of my husband, John Campbell. From the spring day in 2006 that I first floated the idea for this project, through the years that I labored in secret on a venture that alternately invigorated and frustrated me, John's belief in this book and my call to write it never wavered. He brainstormed and prayed with me, read my outlines and rough drafts, talked me through editorial knots and personal doubts, and mixed insightful, unflinchingly honest feedback with constant reminders that a story worth sharing is worth the trouble it takes to tell it. Most crucial during these last few crazy, joyful years, John helped me find the time to write—even when doing so meant more work and less sleep for him. He supported this book and me in every way he could, with a generosity of spirit and constancy of love that still amaze me when I stop to contemplate them. In gratitude for that, and for so much more about John than I could ever adequately express, I dedicate this book to him.

I also want to thank my parents, Tom and Mary Carroll. It is difficult to know where to begin when it comes to thanking the people who gave you life and introduced you to the faith that leads to eternal life, while cheering you through countless challenges along the way. I could thank them for their inspiring example of committed married love, especially in my father's final years, which left an unforgettable legacy for my brother, Tom, and me. I could thank them for their prayers throughout my life, including those my mom offered faithfully for this project and those my dad offered in and through his suffering. Or I could simply say this: I love you both, always.

My agent, Cathy Hemming, was the first person after John to read my manuscript, and her enthusiastic response inspired me to finish it with the sure knowledge that my hidden work had not been in vain. A consummate professional who genuinely delights in her authors, Cathy guided me through the publishing process with skill, perseverance, and good humor. She did so even while coping with the sudden death of her father and new caregiving duties for her mother. I am blessed to have her in my corner.

My editor, Gary Jansen, greeted this manuscript with contagious enthusiasm, immeditately grasping its connection to the "new evangelization" for which we both harbor a passion. He kept that vision in mind while deftly shepherding this book through the day-to-day hurdles of the editorial process. He and the entire team at Image have my gratitude.

Finally, I wish to thank my children: Maryrose, John Patrick, and Clara. You will never know how much you were wanted and how much you are loved, but I hope this book gives you a hint. The only joy sweeter than sharing this journey with your father and you is knowing the eternal embrace of Love that awaits us at our destination. May you live to be saints!

*Colleen Carroll Campbell*
*Eve of the Feast of the Visitation of Mary*
*May 30, 2012*

## READING GUIDE

Questions for Individual or

Group Reflection for

MY SISTERS THE SAINTS

## Chapter 1: Party Girl

1. In this chapter, Colleen discusses her feelings of emptiness and taking her first steps to "open the door to God." What was your first step? What could be your next step toward God?

2. In the anecdote featuring her boyfriend, Colleen realizes that their relationship is actually a "placeholder" for something more satisfying. Have you ever had a placeholder in your life where God should have been? Do you have one now that needs to be surrendered to him?

3. Both Saint Teresa of Ávila and Colleen speak of leading a double life. Neither was living in a conspicuously sinful way, yet they each confessed to the torturous feeling of "living in two worlds." Do you ever feel as though you're living in two worlds, caught between cultural norms and your faith?

## Chapter 2: A Child Again

1. Saint Thérèse of Lisieux wrote about her "little way," which consisted of small, everyday acts of love. These included befriending a particularly cranky nun and not losing patience with others. What are some specific things you could do to

better the lives of those around you, as offerings to God in the "little way"?

2. When Thérèse heard of her father's passing, her reaction was strangely peaceful. How can you find the good—and God's will—in bad tidings?

3. Just as Alzheimer's made Colleen's father more like a child in his faith, Thérèse also strove for childlike faith in God. Why? What qualities do children possess that are essential to your faith?

## Chapter 3: Trust Fall

1. Colleen describes accepting a once-in-a-lifetime opportunity to work as a speechwriter for the president. But this job couldn't fill the ache in her soul for marriage. Have you ever felt the call to sacrifice something important to you for something better? How have you seen the faithfulness of God in that sacrifice?

2. Colleen describes the atmosphere surrounding the speechwriting staff as a "boys' club." Have you ever felt out of place somewhere that you believed God had called you to be? Write out quotes from the saints or Bible verses that remind you of your value to God.

3. Colleen writes that Saint Faustina seemed to embody the verse, "Trust in the Lord with all of your heart and do not

lean on your own understanding (Prov. 3:5)." At the end of this chapter, Colleen realizes that it is not enough to say she trusts in God; she must act as though she does, whether or not she feels it. What's the difference? Are actions or words more important? Why?

## Chapter 4: A Mother at Heart

1. Saint Edith Stein believed that each woman has a maternal spirit. What does that maternal spirit look like in you?

2. Colleen writes about the dark side of a woman's maternal inclinations, when those inclinations are distorted by sin. These negative traits and habits include nagging, manipulation, domineering behavior, and gossip. What are some ways you have seen these weaknesses in yourself? What safeguards can you put in place to curb them?

3. Saint Edith also wrote that "objective work" and daily quiet prayer are twin ways to combat these weaknesses. What are a few concrete ways in which you can apply this doctrine to your own life?

## Chapter 5: Into the Darkness

1. Blessed Mother Teresa of Calcutta wrote about the overwhelming darkness she experienced, even though her entire life was dedicated to God. Despite her desolation, though, she

never faltered in her good work. Is this frightening or reassuring? Why?

2. When speaking of her infertility and waiting to know whether she would ever be a mother, Colleen's mother told her that the waiting itself was her cross to bear. What crosses have you had to bear? Which are you currently bearing? How is God seeing you through?

3. When has God made you wait for something you really wanted? How did the waiting stretch your faith?

## Chapter 6: Triumph of the Cross

1. Colleen writes about how her esteem for Mary grew gradually, and the more she turned to Mary, the more she felt drawn to loving, serving, and imitating her Son, Jesus. In what ways has devotion to Mary led you closer to Christ? In what ways has following Mary's example helped you grow in virtue?

2. Colleen's yearning for motherhood was her own cross to carry, but it also made her dependence on God that much stronger. What trials are you most thankful for? How have they deepened your faith?

3. After having read of Colleen's closeness to six saints, which saints would you like to learn more about, both in reading their works and through prayer?